Straightjacket Memories

Straightjacket Memories

Jonathan Nelson

CROSSBOOKS
PUBLISHING

CrossBooks™
A Division of LifeWay
1663 Liberty Drive
Bloomington, IN 47403
www.crossbooks.com
Phone: 1-866-879-0502

Scripture taken from the New International Version. Copyright 1978, 1983, by
Charles Ryrie, Moody Press Publishing. Used by permission. All rights reserved.

First published by CrossBooks 10/23/2012

ISBN: 978-1-4627-2249-5 (sc)
ISBN: 978-1-4627-2250-1 (e)
ISBN: 978-1-4627-2251-8 (hc)

Library of Congress Control Number: 2012919901

Printed in the United States of America

This book is printed on acid-free paper.
Any people depicted in stock imagery provided by Thinkstock are models,
and such images are being used for illustrative purposes only.
Certain stock imagery © Thinkstock.

BOOK DEDICATION

This book is dedicated to my wife, Alicia. She has been the inspiration in writing Straightjacket Memories. When we took our vows back on August 11th, 2001, she held true to her vow of for better or worse, especially the latter. Through thick and thin she has stood by my side no matter how rough things seemed to be. The Lord knew what He was doing by bringing her into my life because no other woman would have gone through this much just to prove her love to me. She truly is my best friend and my confidant.

A lot of times you hear men complain about their wives to their friends or joke about their relationship to others. I on the other hand, have the upmost respect for my wife and would never belittle her or make light of what she has meant to me in our marriage. Her faith, courage, and dedication to me, has made me into the man I am today.

She has given me three beautiful daughters that make our family complete. I cannot imagine my life without them and feel blessed by God to have them call me their dad. Every time I look into their eyes, I see their mother's goodness in them and her loving spirit.

Failure in this marriage was never an option for my wife. Even when things looked hopeless and the end was in sight, she continued to pray for me and for that day when we could reconcile what had been broken by my terrible disease. I have tried many times to convey to her just how much she means to me but words fall short of how much I truly love her.

Alicia, I love you so much and only you know who I really am. Thank you for never giving up on me or on us. Your faithfulness to me has shown me what it means to truly love someone. You have taught me how to love, how to live, and how to be a godly man. I hope and pray that when you are in need of a hero, I can be the one you turn to. I look forward to the journey and direction our family will take through our Lord and Savior, Jesus Christ.

SPECIAL THANKS

First, I would like to thank my parents (Bruce and Bev) and my sister (Hannah) for believing the best in me even when I could not see it. Also, their emotional support, prayer support, as well as their financial support over these years has helped me write this book.

Next, I would like to thank Marvin Piburn, Jr. M.D. for bringing me back to life. He never once judged me for my awful sins and behavior but rather provided ways to cope through medicine and rational thinking. He and his family have been a blessing to me and their love for my family has been felt.

I would also like to thank Reese Johnson for his financial support. It was through his generous giving which gave us the final approval from God that I was supposed to write this book. Prayers were answered both spiritually and financially through his gift.

I also wish to thank Julie Riley (j.riley creative LLC) for her design of my book cover and to my brother in law, Michael Lu who suggested her talents to me. She turned the ideas I had for the cover into a beautiful imagery of what the book portrays.

Finally, I would like to thank my cousin Barbara Anderson for editing my book and working with me during this long process. Her insight and wisdom helped make this dream of writing my book a reality. She truly was the final piece to the puzzle in putting this entire project together. I am forever indebted to her. Barbara, you have no idea what your work has meant to me. Thank you.

Contents

A LETTER

Dear Friend,

I am thirty-six years old, and I suffer from bipolar disorder. I am the proud father of three girls. My wife Alicia and I have been married for eleven years and are both educators in the public school system. Alicia teaches 4th grade, and I teach physical education and coach boys basketball.

My family and I have been living with my bipolar disorder for the last several years, and it has had a major impact on our family, our professions, and our relationships with others. Because of its impact we believe that we have a story to tell. I have become passionate about telling the story to provide insight into my personal struggle and to provide hope for others who might suffer from the same manic depressive disorder.

Although the story is a personal one, it involves my love of coaching, several teammates, students, family members, friends, and organizations of which I have been and still am a part. I have no desire to harm, discredit, or embarrass these persons or organizations, so all of the names have either been changed or left out of my story.

I was not diagnosed as being bipolar until May 2008, so I spent the first thirty-two years of my life dealing with a very real and powerful force that controlled my life. I didn't know what it was and had no name for it, but it was huge, destructive, and ugly. I came to think of it as a "beast," so that is how I refer to it throughout the story.

I pray that my story will provide you with encouragement if you suffer from bipolar disorder and with understanding if you know someone who is battling with this issue. I trust that it will be a testimony to what the Lord has done in my life and in the lives of those in my family who have been in the struggle with me.

Unworthy, but His,

Jonathan Nelson

Introduction - A Definition

According to Dr. Marv, who is my doctor, my counselor, and friend, bipolar disorder is a serious mental illness influenced by extreme mood swings, from mania to depression. It usually is caused by a chemical imbalance of dopamine, serotonin, and norepinephrine levels in the brain. Research has also shown that there is a probability that this disorder is partially hereditary. It can lead to risky behavior, damaged relationships and careers, and if not treated, can lead to suicidal tendencies.

Bipolar disorder is typically, but not always, seasonal and is patterned by natural sunlight and outdoor temperatures as they shift during the fall and spring equinoxes. During the fall, or autumnal, equinox, the amount of sunlight moves from light to dark, and produces depression in the bipolar person. This depression may last through the fall and into winter when the seasons are cooler. As the amount of light moves from dark to light during the spring, or vernal, equinox, it may produce a manic state which can last from spring into summer when the temperature is warmer. It should be noted that for some who suffer from bipolar disorder, the condition might be reversed in that they experience mania after the fall equinox and depression after the spring equinox. In either instance it is the seasonality that triggers the shift. The pivot points are the equinoxes, and within each equinox there is a peak, or solstice, which often coincides with the peak of mania or depression. The summer solstice typically occurs during late June when there is maximum sunlight followed by maximum heat. The winter solstice usually occurs in late December wherein there is the least amount of sunlight followed by the deepest cold.

There are three types of bipolar disorder. Type I is manic depression wherein a person vacillates, often quickly and unexplainably, between a state of feeling unrealistically invincible and a state of hopelessness so extreme that the only remedy is suicide. The person's "highs," which may lead to psychotic behavior, will last a little over a week at a time while the "lows," which may produce a major depression, will typically last over two weeks.

Type II bipolar disorder is referred to as hypomania. In this type of bipolar disorder, the "highs" are not as severe as in Type I, but they are still intertwined with bouts of severe depression. Typically the "highs" last less than a week; whereas, the "lows" can last well over two weeks.

Type III bipolar disorder is a more mild form called Bipolar "spectrum." Here the mood swings are less severe, alternating between periods of hypomania and mild depression. A person's "highs" and "lows" are shorter in duration but will swing rather frequently and can destroy the way the person functions. Cyclothymia is also associated with Type III bipolar disorder but is a substantially less intense and milder version. People with these last two types of bipolar disorder are often misdiagnosed as having depression alone. This diagnosis creates confusion when a person experiences elevated mood swings.

Bipolar disorder can also manifest itself in what is known as a "mixed state," which consists of the worst parts of mania and the worst parts of depression. In this state manic symptoms would include being euphoric and grandiose, or agitated and angry. The person may experience hallucinations or become delusional, may go on spending sprees or spend inordinate amounts of money on gambling. In this state the mind is racing at such a speed that the person becomes sleep deprived or talks at such a heightened level that the person cannot be understood. Abuse of alcohol and other substances may be evident. Behavior may be impulsive, poorly reasoned (mania) or suicidal (depression).

There are many symptoms of manic depression which can last from a few days up to several months. Manic symptoms can be triggered by such things as a life changing event such as getting married, the loss of a job, the death of a family member and other life altering events; antidepressants; periods of sleeplessness and recreational drug use, and can be exhibited in such behaviors as inflated self-esteem; delusions of grandeur and false beliefs in one's own special abilities; feelings of being above the law; and expectations of perfection. Other common manic symptoms include hyperactivity, increased energy, lack of self-control, racing thoughts, binge eating, drinking or drug use, and the tendency to be easily distracted.

Symptoms of the depressive state of bipolar disorder include daily low moods; low energy levels, difficulty concentrating, remembering, or making decisions; eating disturbances, creating either weight gain or loss; fatigue; feelings of worthlessness, hopelessness, or guilt; loss of self-esteem; persistent sadness and thoughts of death; sleep disturbances; suicidal thoughts; withdrawal from activities that were once enjoyed; and withdrawal from friends and family.

These symptoms are the ones that went undiagnosed and controlled my life for thirty-two years. They created an inner turmoil that paralyzed my every thought, created a world of chaos that affected everyone around me, and brought me to my knees. They became a part of my everyday personality, deteriorating relationships and damaging many things that

I held dear. The turmoil was so brutal and uncivilized that I could only think of it as a beast that was attacking me and that I had no power to fight.

Since at the time many thought that I was struggling with a spiritual issue and that Satan had control of my life, I believe that referring to my struggle with bipolar disorder as "the beast" is appropriate. In the Bible Satan is referred to as a roaring lion ravaging about waiting for those he can destroy, and I am convinced that Satan uses a disease such as bipolar disorder to confuse and destroy those affected by it.

As a Christian I was finding it difficult to find peace with God, and I could not understand anything about God's love while this beast was raging war within me. Although I was baptized and knew that I was a child of God, I wasn't finding any fruit of the Spirit in my life. In fact, I believe that everything about bipolar disorder is "anti-fruit" of the Spirit. Rather than love, joy, peace, long-suffering, kindness, goodness, faithfulness, gentleness, self-control, I was experiencing irritability, reckless behavior, temper tantrums, sleeplessness, elevated moods, gambling sprees, addictions, claustrophobia, severe depression, suicidal thoughts, just to name a few.

These symptoms had appeared at some point or another in my life for many years and, like all who suffer from manic depression, I would go through what is known as rapid cycling. I would be on top of the world one minute and ready to end my life the next. At times there would be episodes where my talents were so brilliantly on display that even I was amazed at what I was able to accomplish. Then at other times I would be so handicapped that I was unable to function at even the most basic level of life.

I had no answers to why I was on this roller coaster other than I knew that I was not living a Christian life and that I was not right with God. My heart wanted to be obedient and to be what God wanted me to be, but "the beast" was crippling every effort. I kept wondering what was wrong with me and why I couldn't be different. Fortunately, for me, I had a concerned family, people who loved me and prayed daily for me. Through God's grace and His answers to prayer, I was properly diagnosed with bipolar disorder and am now, through medication and counseling, able to face "the beast."

I should probably note here that I have been using past tense verbs, as though bipolar disorder is in my past, as though I am now "cured" of this disease and have complete control over "the beast," that he no longer rears his ugly head. That is far from the truth. Bipolar disorder is something that I deal with on a daily basis. Even with the medication, I have to work just to get my kids to daycare and myself to work. It takes a conscious effort to follow through with an entire day of work and daily tasks. There are many days that I struggle to just get out of bed. Each day I have to recognize that I have a choice: I can either live in a world where I feel sorry for myself or grab "the beast" by the horns and deal with it head on.

I was blessed that I was finally diagnosed and am now treating my bipolar disorder. Unfortunately, many others go without diagnosis and are waging a battle that others cannot understand. Society sees them as people with a mental disorder, and automatically assumes that they are unable to function. Society sees them as social misfits and would prefer to have nothing to do with them.

Several years ago, I was talking with a colleague and she said that a guy her daughter is dating is a psycho and that he must be bipolar. I was quietly offended by this statement, yet felt sad that this individual was unaware of what a person who is truly bipolar goes through. Although the person's behavior may not appear rational and even at times bizarre, a person with bipolar disorder is often found to be creatively talented and gifted. People with the disorder excel in various areas and are many times brilliant, yet when it comes to daily routines, they can find themselves lost and unable to perform even the slightest task.

I found this to be true in my case. God blessed me with many talents, especially in the areas of music and athletics. I am an accomplished pianist, violinist, and drummer. I played college basketball where I ended my career as an Academic All-American. Many times I would find myself so wrapped up in my talents that they were used as an escape and a way for me to tune out the pain that I felt in my life. Striving for perfection kept my mind off suicidal and other dark thoughts. I bottomed out when a sports season finished, a piano contest ended, or a violin recital was behind me. It was during this "down" period that people's evaluation of me changed and that I was viewed as someone with a problem. I wanted to tell my colleague that maybe her daughter's friend needed a bit more understanding and that maybe his behavior didn't mean he was a psycho, just that he was having a bad day.

Some doctors have hypothesized that the earth's equinox can have a great effect on someone with bipolar disorder. Their hypothesis stems from the fact that they tend to see more suicides around the spring equinox and more manic behavior in the time of the fall equinox. I am not sure if this hypothesis is true, but I can tell you that the most prevalent time for me to experience mood swings is just before the start of basketball season and directly following it. Basketball season usually begins in October and, depending upon the success of the season, ends in March to early April, directly between the fall and spring equinox. During the season, I am so consumed with practices and games that my "high" lasts all season and depression just isn't a problem. However, once the high ends, so does my control of "the beast"; he rears his ugly head, and I have a major letdown.

In my profession as a coach and teacher, I have kept silent about my disease for fear that people will label me and misunderstand what it is that I go through as a person suffering from bipolar disorder. Many people, like my colleague, associate bipolar disorder with someone who is crazy and who might have violent tendencies. They don't know that when properly medicated a bipolar person can live a normal life. It is true that violent episodes occur, but typically this is due to extreme mood swings or to drug or alcohol abuse. Even then, bipolar people are more likely to be violent toward themselves than to other people.

The underlying problem with mental illness, like bipolar disorder, is that it is not a clear-cut disease like cancer. When people hear of someone diagnosed with cancer, the response is to sympathize and reach out in help and prayer. The reaction to a diagnosis of mental illness is avoidance, fear, and mockery. There is a stigma attached to a person with a mental illness that is not placed upon someone with a physical disease.

Being a person with bipolar disease is much like being the character that Tom Hanks played in the movie *The Castaway*. Their daily struggles are much the same. In the movie, Tom Hanks survives a plane crash and is washed ashore on a deserted island. He does everything in his power to survive, in hopes that one day he would be rescued. The only possession that he has is a locket with his fiancé's picture, which he stares at to keep himself focused on his mission to stay alive. As time passes, packages from the wreckage float to shore and he uses them for survival. His only companion is a volleyball named Wilson.

After a few years he figures a way to construct a sailing vessel that will maneuver him out to sea. In the attempt, he loses Wilson, which causes him to give up, release his oars, and succumb to the sea. In what seems like his final moments of life, a ship rescues him and returns him to his home. Unfortunately, upon his return, he learns that his fiancé has moved on with her life, has married someone else, and is starting a family. Realizing that everything has changed since he has been gone, he returns to his life as a Fed Ex delivery man which results in a new direction and second chance in life.

My battle with bipolar disorder made me feel like I was living on a deserted island. Daily, like Tom Hanks, I sought out moments to hang on to or activities that would help me survive another day, week, or month. "The beast" was so destructive that I was isolated from friends and family. When I had reached the point where it seemed that hope was gone, I was rescued, but upon my return to the real world, I found that my disease had caused so much damage that things would never be the same. However, once I was on medication, I found a new direction, and I was able to start my life over again.

The following poem shows my daily struggle and my hope of victory over "the beast." The following chapters are the story.

VICTORY

Darkness covers my soul within,
The beast destroys my life with sin.
I wake to fight another day,
O Lord please hear me when I pray.
Demons surround me with their hate,
Sinister plans predict my fate.
Suicide thoughts consume my mind,
Reprieve from them I cannot find.
Bipolar in nature is my curse,
Positive thinking I rehearse.
Addictions bring me to my knees,
Those guilty pleasures if you please.
Angels persuade me to break free,
Freedom in Christ so hard to see.
Fruits of the Spirit hard to show,
This disease so strong from below.
My heart doth crave to do what's right,
A hope to see thy glory's light.

My time so brief upon this earth,

To prove His love, a second birth.

Defeat the beast I'll do my best,

A daily grind to pass this test.

This mental illness cripples me,

Brought pain and strife to family.

For in the end this beast will die,

No more weeping, no tears to cry.

Victory in Jesus this battle won,

His kingdom come, His will be done.

Chapter 1 – Opportunity Lost

Although I grew up in a godly home, accepted Jesus as my Lord and Savior at age six, attended a private Christian school from kindergarten through high school, and was very well versed in Scripture, school was somewhat tough for me. Every teacher I had commented on my report cards that I had severe issues with self-control, and as I grew older, because of the school I attended, my lack of self-control was believed to be a "fruit of the Spirit" issue. I suppose that if I were in school today, I would have been diagnosed with Attention Deficit Hyperactivity Disorder and treated accordingly, but when I was growing up the medical field was prescribing Ritalin to students who were hyperactive. Ritalin is a type of amphetamine with serious side effects and caused much controversy among the medical field and parents. Because of the controversy over Ritalin, my parents decided that the side effects were not worth the risk, tried different avenues for me to deal with my hyperactivity, and I was left being labeled a kid with a lack of self-control.

My passion growing up was sports, primarily basketball. My parents, however, were music teachers and wanted me to master the fine arts, so I started playing the piano and violin at a very early age. Fortunately for me, my parents allowed me to participate in both athletics and the fine arts: I just had to practice the piano and violin before I could go out and shoot hoops. That made all three of us happy.

I worked very hard through my early years to be the best that I could be in whatever I attempted. I became ultra-competitive and found most of my self-worth by winning competitions and being judged the best. My training in music and athletics was so intense on all levels and my self-esteem so attached to it that I refused to fail at anything I did. I did well in school, but I excelled in music and athletics. Because of my talents and gifts I was admired as a prodigy in some circles and hated because of them in others. The harder I strove for approval to gain self-esteem, the more I drove my friends away with my success.

While trying to find a balance in these areas, I was dealing with another issue that affects so many adolescents in middle school, but it seemed especially difficult for me because of my issue with self-esteem and the approval of others. I had developed a severe case of acne which would last well into my early college days and was so debilitating that I didn't want to be seen in public. In fact, it was so bad that one day a girl whom I had been attracted to for some time in middle school came up to me and said, "You would be really cute if you'd just wash your face and get rid of all those zits." What she didn't realize was that I was probably the cleanest kid in the entire country because when I wasn't practicing or shooting hoops, I was scrubbing my face to get rid of the acne. My acne had nothing to do with personal hygiene but rather with a chemical imbalance that set off my oil glands. I was on different types of antibiotics and creams to help control outbreaks, but they did very little to help my complexion. The comment from my classmate and the acne itself made me think that I was not good enough in and of myself, so the only way that I could gain the approval of others was to try even harder at winning music contests and being a star on the basketball court.

My desire and dedication to be the best helped me as a freshman to be a starter on the varsity team, but instead of the popularity I had hoped for, I encountered more jealousy. Nevertheless, my zeal for being the best in the game was enhanced when my parents took me to the state basketball tournament at the end of my freshman season. It was a perfect trip, and I realized that the state tournament was the stage for the entire state to see the talents of the best players and teams. The experience motivated me even more to be the best player I could be to ensure that someday I would be on the floor at the state basketball tournament playing for the championship.

It was during this time, while I was working so hard for approval from all around me, that I began to have bouts with depression. My success in music contests and competitions was driving my classmates further away, and although I was a "super hero" to the media sports world, when the season ended, my world came to a crashing halt. As a result, I would have episodes of anger at home where I would punch holes into the dry wall and listen to violent music just to release pent-up frustration.

During my sophomore year, I had a very successful individual campaign, averaging over seventeen points per game, but our team always fell short in tournaments. Because of this, as in my freshman year, I fell into a deep depression once the season was over. At the time I figured that I was just going through what every athlete goes through after a disappointing end of the season. I had no idea that there was something sinister at work inside of me, growing stronger at the end of each successive basketball season. I began having more arguments with my family and taking my frustrations out in more violent ways. At the same time I was confronting the fact that I was not being the Christian that I had been brought up to be and my love for others was simply nonexistent. Fortunately for me, rather than turning to drugs or alcohol as many teens do, I escaped the depression by focusing on working harder and harder at my music and basketball. At least, I thought, these were more positive ways of releasing my emotions and certainly less destructive to myself and my family. My whole focus was on my junior season, making sure that it would be a special one, and it was.

The regular season ended with the conference championship game against a team whom we had beaten by seventeen points rather easily earlier in the season in their home gym. We were fairly confident of a game on our own court, so we were in disbelief when we faced a two-point deficit with only eighteen seconds remaining and the conference championship on the line. The player from the opposing team had made the first of two free throws, leaving us trailing by three points. We knew that we needed a miracle. We got the rebound after the second missed free throw, but when the ball was passed to me at the top of the key, I lost the grip on the ball for a brief second. After pulling myself together, turning to square up, I launched a three-point shot from about twenty-two feet. The ball grabbed the side of the rim, and curled in with seconds to spare to tie the game.

The crowd erupted, my body went completely numb, and my only thought was that we had to stop our opponents from hitting a game-winning shot at the buzzer. There was a pass from the top of the key and the opposing post player ran over our big man to make the basket. Luckily the official called an offensive foul and the game went into overtime. I was overcome with excitement to realize that I had hit the shot to send the game into overtime and to know that we had the momentum now to finish the job.

We took control early in overtime, but they fought back hard, forcing me to make two free throw shots and give us a four-point advantage with just seconds remaining in overtime. Our opponents managed to hit a three-point shot to end the game, but we had won by one point! The celebration began, and we staked our claim to an outright conference championship with a team of juniors in our first year in the conference.

The success of the conference game and the way we were playing made me realize that we had a great chance to make it to the state tournament. We were clicking on all cylinders. There was no jealousy, no animosity, and no chemistry issues on the team. We were just that, a team! We all knew our jobs and each one performed to perfection night in and night out. My dream was clearly in reach!

The excitement and satisfaction of winning the conference game didn't last long, however. We had one game to play before districts, and although we won by sixteen points in a very hostile environment, I had not played my best game. The "beast" seemed to always make his presence known in times when I hadn't performed up to the standards that I had set for myself. The mistakes that I made, whether in musical performance or in athletics, always made me feel guilty, that

I let my teammates or coaches or teachers down, which made it very hard for me to feel positive about the event or to congratulate my teammates or fellow contestants. Rather, I wanted to pull away and be by myself. So on a night when I should have been really pumped, I felt discouraged and depressed.

The coach gave us the next couple days off to enjoy the success of our regular season and to rest up for the following week when we would begin district play. Because of the way teams were chosen for district play, we found ourselves playing the first round against a neighboring school that was ranked with us in the top ten. In addition, we were to play the game on our opponent's home court, which made the game even more challenging. Nevertheless, our record of only one loss on the road made us confident that we could play anyone, anytime, anywhere. We had no idea of the very real challenge that we would soon be facing.

After practice just one week before the first district game, a friend and teammate asked me and another friend to go with him to watch a game at another high school in town. Because of homework and being tired from practice, we chose to stay home, study, and watch basketball on television.

Later that evening we missed a phone telling us that Steve had been in a car accident on his way home from the game. His car was hit on the passenger side and sent careening into the ditch on the opposite side of the road. Any passengers in the car with him would have been killed immediately.

I heard about the accident on the radio the next morning while I was getting ready for school. My dad rushed me over to the hospital where other teammates had already gathered. We learned that Steve was in very serious condition and in a coma. He suffered from a collapsed lung, bone contusions, and a compound fracture in his right thigh from the impact of the stick shift during the crash. He was on a ventilator to help him breathe and only his family was allowed to see him.

Any thoughts of basketball and the upcoming district game were far from our minds. While waiting to hear news, we prayed for God to lay his healing hand on Steve, to give the doctors wisdom and skill, and to give his family comfort and strength. Steve's dad told us that since there was nothing we could do, we should maybe try to go to school to keep our minds off things and that he would keep us informed.

A few close friends on the team knew that school would be difficult for us, so we decided to just hang out together, talk about what would happen next, and how we should respond with our other teammates when we resumed practice. We talked to our coach and decided that rather than practicing that night we would spend the time at the hospital with family and friends.

We always broke huddle with shouting, "Glory to God," but never did it mean more to me than during the time we spent together that night at the hospital. For the first time in my life, basketball became secondary, and my thoughts were on God and my friend. My prayers were not for success on the court and doing my best but were for healing for my friend. I was thankful for the flowers and support from everyone who visited and thankful that as a team we were able to be a testimony to our trust that God was in control and that He held us all in His hands.

It was difficult to be in school the next day, but when Steve's father showed up during practice, we learned that Steve was improving but would be out the rest of the season. He also told us that he knew that Steve would want us to prepare hard for district and to play to our very best. We missed Steve but were determined to win the game for him. We practiced that week harder than we had ever practiced before.

Steve's health improved during the week before district play, and he had come out of the coma. Knowing this, I went back into basketball mode and the "beast" was in full attack. I was on such a high that I thought I could do anything and that I could almost single-handedly win the game. However, deep down I knew that it was going to take a special effort from my teammates as well if we were going to win against a quality team like the opponents we were facing.

The morning of the game, our coaches took another friend and me to the hospital to see Steve. It was a shock to see him attached to so many machines and tubes, but when we stood next to his bed and held his hand, we clearly heard him say, "Win." Statistically, he was our second leading scorer and our leading rebounder. Obviously, we were missing a big piece of our team, but I believed that the team could step up our game enough to make up for Steve's absence. Throughout the remainder of the day, I was convinced that God was going to give us a win after everything we had been through and that He would direct the rest of the tournament to get us to state.

The trip to the game was only about fifteen minutes, but you could hear a pin drop as each member of the team was in his own world of thought focusing on the task at hand. When we arrived at the game, we were surrounded by fans who had shown up early and by the media which had taken a special interest in the game because of its being a district game between two highly ranked schools and because of Steve's accident. Television stations and newspaper writers were on hand to see how the absence of a valued teammate would affect our game. We quickly moved through the crowd: we had business to attend to, and I was not about to get sidetracked.

In the locker room the only sound was that of ankles being taped and buttons of warm-up suits being snapped. Coach did not give a long speech since there was no need for words at this point. In the huddle we looked at each other and said," Let's play hard for Steve. Win or lose, leave it all out there for him!"

We entered the gymnasium to the sound of one thousand cheering fans, all wearing the same buttons with Steve's name and number on them that were on our warm-ups. It was a standing-room-only crowd, and I knew it was going to be a big night for our school, for the team, for Steve, and most of all, for me. The "beast" was hungry for success, and I was going to feed it.

In the first quarter we managed to keep close to our hard-hitting opponents, and trailed by only a few points through the second quarter. As half time approached, I hit a fade away three-point shot on the sideline inbound play with two defenders flying at me to cut the deficit to a single digit. As we ran to the locker room, we felt that we had momentum on our side and believed that we had a chance to make a run in the second half.

Although we scored the first few points of the second half to keep the score close, our opponents were on fire. In the end, we lacked the power to beat a team that eventually went on to win the state championship. It was hard to have our season end in this manner, and it was difficult to walk through the line shaking hands with the winning team. I knew many of the players on this team, and some of them were good friends, so I knew that my testimony had to be strong even though all I wanted to do was cry.

All of my teammates felt the same. We shed many tears in the locker room over what had probably been the worst week of many of our lives. Just a week and a half earlier we had been celebrating a conference championship and Steve was with us, healthy and whole. Things had taken a one hundred and eighty degree turn. Coach didn't have much to say other than to keep our heads up, that he was proud of the way we had conducted ourselves during a very trying time, and that we had shown a lot of character and dignity in our loss of the game.

I didn't need to hear that right then because our season was over, and my friend was still in the hospital. Rather than showering and leaving, I yelled, "This will NOT happen next year! We work harder and we get even more serious about our senior year!" After that we quickly dressed and headed for the bus. The long road to recovery for Steve and our team had begun.

In the next few weeks and months, the "beast" took over my thinking. I just could not understand why God had allowed this to happen. Why would He take Steve away from us and then leave us hung out to dry in the first round of districts? Some people outside of my family whom I loved and trusted suggested that maybe it was sin in Steve's life or our lives that caused both the accident and the loss. The "beast" took that idea and hammered me with the thought that it was all my fault because I knew that I was not a perfect person. I knew that all people sin and that sin was a part of our fallen nature. I also knew that I had confessed my sin and that I was a born again Christian, but the "beast" continued to remind me of past sins which would throw me into bouts of depression. At the time people, including my family, thought that my depression was the result of the accident, the loss of the district game, and that basketball season was over. Little did anyone know the toll that the "beast" was taking on my life and that I had no control over it.

We had a great time at camp that summer for several reasons: Steve was making a rapid recovery; the team was growing together; and lives were changing as a result of some revival services we had attended at a nearby church. I felt that the Lord was working and that the "beast" was getting a little quieter. I was confident that the following year would be a good one for me and the team.

Unfortunately, the good feeling did not last long. On the way home the "beast" started having a field day reminding me that the coach had not really reinforced my efforts at camp. The "beast" pointed out that the team had started to act a bit cooler towards me and coach had been exceptionally hard on me at camp. When we arrived home, my parents noticed my discontent with the team and asked about my attitude. I just told them that I had been voted MVP at camp, showed them my trophies and awards, and said that I was tired.

We were so excited after camp that when school started we didn't think that basketball season would ever arrive. When it did come, however, I had to face a reality that was hard for me to swallow. During the first week of practice, Coach named someone else as sole captain of the team. I felt that I had the same leadership qualities as the other person, but when the coach mentioned spiritual leadership, the "beast" made me feel as if the coach was saying that my spirituality was a quality I was lacking and was what kept me from being at least a co-captain for the year. When we were dismissed from practice, I made my way outside and vomited in the bushes. I used that as an excuse to go home so that I did not have to spend any more time with the team. The rest of the week I tried to prove to myself, the team, and the coach that I could be a leader even without the title.

The remainder of the week in practice, I was apprehensive about asserting myself offensively, and my shooting was off. The coach's frustration with me only made it worse, and the "beast" was laughing at me, which drove me in a depression that would eventually make me physically sick. I didn't want my emotions to make me a detriment to the team, so I simply told the coach that I was battling the flu.

To help myself overcome my disappointment and depression, I used the excitement of our first game against our archrivals, and, along with the team, walked into the gym with confidence. We came out hungry for victory, and at one point in the first half we led by twenty points. We went into the locker room at half time with a fourteen point lead only to have the coach tell me that I needed to step up my game and that I wasn't into it mentally. He then changed our strategy from an attacking man-to-man defense full court, which had gotten us a big lead, to a match-up zone defense just to take our opponents off guard. I wanted to speak up, but I wasn't the captain and kept quiet. The team looked to our captain to speak up, but he said nothing. I couldn't believe it!

The "beast" took over in the second half of the game. It kept reminding me that I wasn't captain and that I wouldn't be able to make a shot no matter how hard I tried. I barely scored a point after scoring ten in the first half. After the game, the coach came up to me and asked, "What is your problem, Nelson?" I didn't respond, and he went on to point out the sin in our lives. I knew there were several guys not living the life God had called us to live, but I was not a part of some of the extra-curricular activities that coach was alluding to. Even though I didn't feel that the coach was talking to me directly, the "beast" had a great time because guilt had always been a problem for me. I felt that I was right with God, but I was struggling with something that I couldn't understand. I just knew that it was taking over my life, and I didn't know what to do about it.

The "beast was using the fact that I was not captain of the team to destroy my love of basketball and my relationship with the guys on the team. When I met up with our team captain later that week, I told him how I felt. I told him that I was okay with his being captain, but couldn't understand why I was not sharing the position with him. He agreed with me about the situation, which helped me to face the next game. Not only was I able to score twenty-seven points that night, but I felt good about overcoming my attitude of rejection. Nevertheless, the "beast" continued to haunt me about my leadership skills and my seeming lack of importance to the team.

I was so worn down by my battle with the "beast," that by Christmas break I had mononucleosis and spent most of the holiday vacation in bed. What practices I did attend took such a toll on me physically that all I could do after them was sleep for hours. I kept thinking that if I could just get healthy, things would be better and that I would be able to start fresh and could turn things around for me and my team.

We rattled off some rather easy victories until late January when we had another match up with an opponent we had played earlier in the season. Our opponents had been rolling through teams as though nothing could stop them, and neither could we. We lost by seven points, and I was angry and frustrated.

It appeared that our team had lost the confidence and chemistry that had made us successful in the past. Our captain had developed a more offensive mind set, our posts were upset that they were not getting the ball, while I, on the other hand, was afraid of doing anything that would let my coach down. The only silver lining was that we were to play this same opponent in the first round of districts, and we firmly believed in the theory that it is tough to defeat a team three times in the same season. I believed that our first two losses to this team were so that we would win the one game that mattered. Our sights were set on beating this team more than ever in districts because the winner of the first round would have an easy road to the state tournament.

While I was busy focusing on games and we were in the midst of a winning streak, my dad and my coach were discussing my attitude, my less-than-stellar performance on the court, and what to do to move things in a positive direction. It was at my coach's request that he meet with my dad since he was genuinely concerned about what was going on with me. My coach was shocked to learn that not naming me as a captain of the team had completely demoralized me because I had worked very hard to please him and earn his praise. Another problem was that I had not been playing much because we were beating teams by an average margin of thirty points and the bench players were being brought into the game. My father told the coach that my value as a team member might be lost for the remainder of the season.

My battle with my emotions wasn't helped when in the first round of districts the coach did not have me guarding their best player. It had been my job to guard the best players throughout my basketball career, and I was good at it! The coach's decision only fueled the "beast," and my confidence was being quickly ripped to shreds. I began to think that I couldn't even play the game, especially in this particular gym. I was extremely frustrated because I had been taken from a routine position and placed in an unfamiliar situation. Ironically, I ended up breaking the school scoring record in that game, but it didn't matter because we lost the game and, consequently, our berth in the state tournament. I was frustrated with myself and everyone who was a part of the team. I felt that the only dream I had ever hoped to fulfill was destroyed. All of those hours, camps, and years of spending time in the gym were for nothing.

When I got home that night, the "beast" was unleashed. I punched the wall, threw things, and swore up and down the hallway in front of my parents. I was convinced by the "beast" that my life and future had been stolen from me. I had had my problems with people from time to time, but until that night, I had never hated anyone. That night, I was filled with hatred. After a time, I was able to calm down and get some rest, but the remainder of the year I was consumed by the loss and in deep depression that I had fallen short of my best.

My parents had always been my biggest fans, had always supported me in whatever I tried, and pushed me to be the best I could be. So, naturally, they were upset with the district loss and also thought that something had been stolen from me. However, they knew that it wasn't the state tournament dream that had been stolen, but that something innate within me had been wrenched away at a horrible cost. They just had no idea what it was.

We struggled together for the remainder of my senior year, and somehow I manage to graduate. I didn't like my senior year, so I was glad it was over and that I could put all of my bad feelings and disappointing memories behind me. I had a new goal. I was going to college and was going to play basketball! Playing basketball was all that I every really wanted to do, and I was trying hard not let my feelings about my senior season get in the way. In fact, I was even going to attend my coach's alma mater, a school that I had signed with during Christmas break of my senior year because of my respect for him. AND I was going to win a National Championship!

Chapter 2 -
On My Own

I was nervous, scared, and excited during the fourteen-hour drive to the school I had chosen to attend for the next four years. I had never been away from my family for more than a week at any given time, so I was homesick for them before they had even left the parking lot and wondered if I had made the right decision about college. The only thing that made me feel at all better was that I was away from the situation that had been making life hard for me the previous few years, and I took comfort in the fact that maybe, just maybe, I had left the "beast" at home. Unfortunately, he travels with me wherever I go; college was no exception. College just presented new and different challenges, and being on partial scholarships for both basketball and piano didn't help.

Although the school I had chosen was an independent Christian university, it was associated with a church body, and the rules and regulations we were required to follow were mandated by the church organization. The church and, consequently, the university had a very legalistic belief about sin. The atmosphere at the university was very judgmental, dictated a worship philosophy and style that was very different from the one in which I had been raised, and mandated that students attend church services on campus on a rigid weekly schedule.

The impact of this type of spiritual teaching was intended, I think, to make students acknowledge their human condition and to seek a cleansing from the sinfulness. The philosophy, however, seemed to me to be centered on rules, restrictions, mandates, and punishment rather than on man's free will and on God's grace. It appeared to me that they were teaching that man is saved by church attendance and obedience to institutional standards. I had never been taught that what I did or didn't do according to the world's dictates had anything to do with my salvation or God's forgiveness of sin. I believed that I should be obedient to God's will because of what Christ had accomplished on the cross for me, so being required to attend a particular church and to worship in a particular manner resulted in anger and emotional stress. The "beast" was on the prowl again. He had simply chosen a different venue. Now I was being judged in a church pew rather than on a basketball court or on a concert stage. Once again I was trying to be the best I could be and, according to the school and church, I was failing miserably.

The daily atmosphere on campus caused me to feel extreme guilt, and the internal struggle was excruciating. In one instance, I was made to feel that my salvation was in doubt because I used an NIV Bible in class rather than the King James. At other times, I was afraid that if I didn't spend Monday nights going door to door handing out tracts that I would be condemned to hell. If students missed church, chapel, Sunday school, or simply left a little trash in the dorm trashcan, they were given demerits. If one earned enough demerits, the student would be grounded on campus for the weekend, and if the demerits continued to mount, one would be expelled from the school. The "beast" was using these fears to the point that if this is what I had to worry about or do to be a Christian, I didn't want to have anything to do with it.

The only thing that helped me cope and persevere was my passion to play basketball. Preseason practice was grueling, but I was there to compete, and if I wanted a starting position on the team I had to work for it. My determination earned me two black eyes and a bloody lip in just the first month of practice. Unfortunately, my effort seemed to be for naught when I didn't score any points in the first scrimmage, and I began to think that I was not college basketball material. I wanted to simply quit and go home, but my dad convinced me to give it another week and said that if I still felt defeated, he would come get me.

The following week our scrimmage was against a highly respected junior college team. In that game I scored thirty-two points and regained my confidence on the court. I felt that I had conquered the "beast" who just a week before had me discouraged and ready to throw in the towel, literally and figuratively. Sadly, though, the "beast" was not finished with me and stood ready to attack on several levels.

I continued to practice hard, and five games into the season I had a breakthrough night that proved I deserved to be a starter, a position I would maintain for the remainder of the season. My newly gained confidence and my personal success didn't translate into team success, however. We were losing more that we were winning, and it was very hard for me to handle since I had never been on a losing team before. I just trusted that the excitement of tournament would turn us into a Cinderella team and maybe we would have a shot at making it to the National Tournament.

Despite my enthusiasm and proven skills, I was benched in favor of an older player because the coach thought that youth was inexperienced in tournament play and wouldn't be able to handle the pressure of playing against the teams with whom we might be seeded. The "beast" was enjoying my frustration and fueled my anger at being replaced by a player whom I believed was inferior to me in skill and performance. I did, however, get to play in the game for a short time before being pulled, for whatever reason, and sat out the remainder of the game. We ended up losing the game and ended the season with an eleven and sixteen record. I was disgusted because even though I had had a good year, the "beast" was making me feel as though I had screwed up and would never get it together.

Added to my frustration with basketball was my frustration about my relationship with a girl I had started dating early in my freshman year. In the beginning the relationship was progressing well, but the rules on campus didn't make it easy to see each other, and the teaching about dating kept us from getting to know each other in a healthy way. Students under the age of twenty weren't allowed to single date, and I was only eighteen. In order to see each other, we had to sneak off campus. I didn't think that the dating rule made any sense because I had been single dating for a while in high school. Nevertheless, breaking the rule made me feel guilty, so when we did finally get to spend time together, the atmosphere was tense and uncomfortable rather than relaxing and enjoyable.

The "beast" was interfering in this relationship by convincing me that rather than having any real affection for me, my girlfriend was with me only because she was rebelling against her upbringing and the school rules. These feelings, coupled with my depression over basketball, began to have a very negative effect on my attitude and behavior around my girlfriend. The "beast" was using these feelings to push my girlfriend away and to add even more confusion and fear to my life. I began to think, say, and do things that I had no control over. I was beaten up emotionally, physically, and spiritually, and was even contemplating suicide.

The last month of school was extremely difficult as I found it harder and harder to control the "beast" and to keep my thoughts and feelings to myself. In one of these instances, my girlfriend tried to stop me from saying what was probably a little over the top to some Bible students who stopped us on our way to church one Sunday morning.

In trying to stop me, my girlfriend grabbed my arm, an action that was witnessed by a resident assistant. The school had a rule against public display of affection, so we were given ten demerits. My girlfriend had by this time accrued enough demerits that she was "dismissed" from school the following week, and I was informed that if I was caught being seen with her, I would be removed from school indefinitely as well. I couldn't afford to be kicked out of school, and I didn't want to give up my relationship with my girlfriend, so we continued to see each other but had to be very careful to hide it. The fact that her home was close to the college we attended made it easy to meet on the fly, but the secrecy and lying didn't help our relationship.

I was more than ready for the semester to end so that I could go home and maybe gain a new perspective on the year, my relationship with my girlfriend, and my spiritual situation.

Most importantly, I hoped to gain control of my battle with the "beast."

The "beast," however, was not quite ready to surrender. He wanted to get in one more strike before I headed home for the summer. Because the "beast" thrives on impulse rather than reasoning, I decided not to have my girlfriend take me to the airport. Instead I got a ride from another girl. This girl was merely a good friend, but my girlfriend was very suspicious of this arrangement and became extremely jealous and angry. We decided to end our relationship.

Chapter 3 –
The Legalistic Shocker

Being home for a few months in the summer was good therapy for me. I had a chance to relax and also to play some basketball in a midnight league that was helping keep athletes off the streets. Because I wasn't really competing in this league, I could work on my game without a lot of tension or demands placed on me, and that summer I played at a level that I had never played before. When it was time to return to campus, I was excited to get back and felt mentally able to tackle some of the "non-basketball" issues that had plagued me my freshman year.

Sadly, on my first night back on campus, I was confronted with the legalistic philosophy that had frustrated me a year earlier. My buddy and I arrived in town on a Sunday evening and thought that if we didn't unpack, shower, and change clothes, we would be in time for church services. We should have remembered that the shorts, sandals, and t-shirt that my friend had on were not in line with the campus church dress code, but we didn't, and we sat in back of the church trying to be inconspicuous. It didn't take long for someone to approach us about our attire, and we tried to explain that we had just driven fourteen hours and would have been late for church if we had stopped to change clothes. The man told us that if we were devout Christians we would have planned better and been appropriately dressed for worship. I ignored the comment, but my friend stupidly retorted that nobody judged Jesus for wearing sandals. We were then escorted out of the church and told never to come to church dressed like that again. I realized that I was back in the oppressive environment that I had been free of during the summer, and I could feel "the beast" awakening.

After that incident school rolled along quite nicely for a while. I seemed to get along well with everyone on campus and had a new roommate who immediately felt like a brother to me. I was in great shape during preseason workouts, my confidence was high, and I was playing better than ever. And I was playing more than ever. I was enjoying playing so much that even after three-hour practices and scrimmages, my roommate and I would go back at night to play in open gym with other guys on campus.

I was also feeling good about my spiritual life. I was diving into Scripture, studying passages in church, chapel, and Sunday school. All the pieces of my life seemed to be coming together, and I was living the life that I had dreamed I would live. But dreams are dreams; they come to an end, and reality takes their place.

During the fall I had started dating a girl whom I enjoyed spending time with because, unlike other girls, she understood my commitment to basketball, and, even though she wanted to spend more time with me, she realized that I needed to focus on my game. We decided that our relationship would be as friends and nothing more. We called each other frequently and emailed back and forth.

One night while we were e-mailing and having fun with the new computer system, I received a random message from a guy named Joe. He started asking questions about my "girlfriend" and said that he was interested in dating her. At first I was a little jealous because I had dated her and really appreciated our friendship, but then I realized that I had no claim on her since we were no longer dating. I answered the questions politely, told him that I thought she was a wonderful girl and that if it weren't for the time I needed to devote to basketball, I would be seeing her on a more serious basis.

At that time he started making more negative comments about my relationship with her, asked if we had had sex, and implied that he was going to take advantage of the fact that she and I were "just friends" and ask her out. I liked and respected her very much, so I felt protective of her and warned him to be careful of the way he treated her and of any intentions he might have in regard to her. He said that there was nothing I could do about it and that if I tried to stop him from dating her he could ruin my life. I was ready to take a swing at him, but I knew that one punch to his face could have serious consequences to my basketball career. So I reined in "the beast" and simply told him that I expected him to treat her in the way that she deserved, with respect and dignity. Later in the week when she asked my advice about going out with Joe, I told her to be careful, to use her best judgment, and that I trusted her.

Late Sunday night when I called her to ask her how the date went, she was very distant and not as talkative as she usually was. I tried to get her to tell me what was bothering her, but she kept changing the topic or interrupting our conversation to talk to her roommate. In the middle of our talk, my phone beeped, but by the time I had switched to answer, the caller had hung up. Rather than hanging up when I told her I had another call, she had simply laid her phone down. I tried to get her attention, but she couldn't hear me, so I waited for her pick the phone back up. In the meantime, I could hear her sobbing to her roommate and learned that Joe had made inappropriate advances to her. Her admission that she might have led him on didn't excuse his behavior, and I was furious.

Apparently Joe had been busy that weekend because almost as soon as I had hung up the phone, two other guys came to my room and told me that Joe had attempted the same thing with their girlfriends that weekend. Of course, we all wanted to find Joe and beat him up, but instead we went to his room to talk to him and tell him that we knew what he had done and that we would not tolerate his actions towards these girls.

Joe's response was to smirk and laugh at us. He believed that there was nothing we could do to stop him. Not thinking, I reminded him that I had sold knives during the summer to make extra money and that if he had a problem keeping his hands to himself that I could fix his problem. I meant it as a joke, and we went back to our rooms believing that we had made our point with him. Little did I know how that "joke" would change my life forever.

The next Tuesday morning I was awakened by a knock on my door. Thinking that it was just one of the guys coming to hang out, I turned over and tried to go back to sleep. After a brief moment or two I heard a key in the lock and turned back to see our resident director coming into the room. He told me that the Dean of Men wanted to see me. I thought that a bit odd and was quite surprised to find myself being escorted to the Dean of Students office by all of the male resident assistants. By this time I was wide awake and remembered what had transpired over the weekend. I assumed that this meeting had something to do with that, but innocently believed that Joe was the one in trouble and that I was just being called in to corroborate the girls' stories.

Obviously I was very surprised to learn that I was being accused of bullying Joe and of threatening him with a knife. When I tried to explain what had happened, they told me that someone had overheard the conversation in Joe's room that night and had reported it to the Dean. I told them that I was not threatening Joe, but wanted him to seriously think about the way he was affecting my friend and the other girls and that he should respect their purity. They ignored my explanation and blamed my attitude toward Joe on the fact that he was dating a girl I had previously dated. Consequently, they accused me of being the ring leader of the group. I was dumbfounded to the point that "the beast" itself stayed quiet. All I had tried to do was keep a girl from being taken advantage of, and I was now the bad guy.

After two hours of questioning, the Dean of Men took me to lunch. I felt like a criminal who had to be escorted for fear I would escape. However, I felt a huge sense of relief when the lunch conversation centered on basketball. We talked about my game and that he had heard that I was going to be one of the keys to the upcoming season. I began to feel like I would get a slap on the wrist and all would be over.

I couldn't have been more wrong. When we arrived back at the Dean's office, I saw that my coach had been brought in and that I now had to tell the whole story again to him.

I tried to explain my actions and why I had said what I did, but the Dean kept interrupting. He insisted that what I had done was unscriptural and that God was very displeased with me. In the beginning Coach seemed to be very confused and attempted to defend me, but when his loyalty to the school and his Christianity was challenged, Coach caved to their argument. He agreed with them when they said that being an athlete didn't grant me the privilege of intimidating another student. My heart was in my throat and panic began to set in when Coach left the room without acknowledging me.

When I saw Joe and both of our resident assistants go in to see the Dean, my frustration and panic started to turn to anger. I started punching my thighs and "the beast" arrived to keep me company. I tried to remain calm when Joe was dismissed and I was called back in to the room. By this time we had spent nine hours in questioning, explanations, and discussions. I was ready for it to end, but I wasn't prepared for what happened next. The Dean of Men looked me straight in the eye, and without a hint of compassion or regret, said "Jon, we have given this a lot of thought and prayer. We feel it is in the best interest of the school, Joe, and the student body that you be dismissed from this institution."

I felt the tears stream down my face and all I could think about was what I would tell my family. How would they ever understand? The anger that had consumed me just a few moments earlier drained from by body, and I remained motionless, just letting the tears fall. I had just been kicked out of school for defending a girl's honor. I had done what I thought God wanted me to do, and now I felt that He was deserting me.

When I called my parents to tell them, I expected that they would be very upset and disappointed in me. Instead, they were angry at the school and its decision and told me that they were coming down immediately to help me fight. Dad then called my coach to get his opinion and advice and learned that Coach didn't know about my dismissal. Coach told my dad that he would go over to the dorm to talk to me. I was comforted knowing that people were helping me rather than condemning me for something that I did not intend to do.

Coach didn't say much when he first arrived; he just grabbed a chair and sat with me for a while. When he finally talked he told me that he was in my corner and supported me one hundred percent. I began to think that things would be okay. He listened to my side of the story and thought that my punishment was harsh and undeserved. He told me that I had done a noble thing but that I probably should have chosen different words. When I left I told him that my parents were coming to help me fight the decision. That night I was able to get some rest because I knew that help was on its way.

I was very happy to see my parents the next day and learn that they had set up a meeting with the president of the school for late in the afternoon. When we arrived on campus, I was greeted by many students who told me that they were praying for me and believed that I stood a chance of getting the decision reversed. Their support and the fact that my parents were walking beside me gave me confidence as we entered the president's office and took our seats.

The president had not yet heard the whole story and had been informed only that I had threatened a student with a knife. When I had a chance to tell him what had happened, he admitted that the story had been misconstrued to the point of making a bad situation horrifying. He agreed that something had to be done to stop Joe, but also believed that I had overstepped my boundaries in the way that I had dealt with it. He said that his job was to protect the students at the school and that my actions and threats could have harmed another student. Apparently the girl's safety didn't matter to him. However, when my mother told him that she would hold him personally responsible if anything happened to the girls involved because no one had listened to me, he was flustered for the rest of the meeting.

After an hour or so of discussion and wavering back and forth, the president decided that I could be reinstated but that I would have to face some form of punishment because students can't go around threatening other students and possibly putting lives in danger. He said that he needed to talk to a few people and meet with some personnel before making any final decision and that he would call us at the hotel the next morning with his final decision.

We were relieved that I was going to be back in school, and I was looking forward to getting back to working with my team. Our relief turned to frustration the next morning when the phone call didn't come. My parents were concerned about getting back to work but didn't want to leave if more help was needed. They finally decided to stay regardless of the outcome, and when the phone call came late that afternoon, I was really glad they did.

I listened to my dad's side of the conversation and was feeling that everything was going to be fine until my dad shouted, "You can't do that to him! This has nothing to do with basketball!" After another minute or two my dad told the president that we would need to think about what was now on the table and get back to him. I could tell by the look on Dad's face that I was not going to like what I was going to hear. The president's decision was that they were going to reverse the dismissal but that I would be suspended from basketball for the first semester. For me that was the worst possible punishment. Yes, I knew that I was in college for an education, but all I wanted to do was play basketball and now I couldn't. At that point "the beast" was unleashed. I ranted and raved my way around the hotel room, screaming that I would never accept that decision and that I would simply drop out of school right then and there.

My dad was more rational and suggested that we call my coach and get his opinion about the number of games I would miss and how that would affect my season. When I learned that I would miss ten games, I knew that I had been moved from a starting position to having to work my way back into the rotation after Christmas break, and I didn't think I had the strength to do that. It had been a horrible week, and I didn't think I could face sitting out the semester. Coach urged me to think about it and said that we might be able to get the punishment reduced or waived with good behavior on my part. I decided to not make a decision that night, to talk it over with my folks, and to come to some conclusion by the next day.

We went to brunch the next morning and went round and round about what I should do. On the one hand going home and starting over was very appealing after everything I had been through. On the other hand, I didn't want to let my coach or the team down. "The beast" had a say also by telling me that I was a quitter and didn't deserve a chance at an education or a basketball career. "The beast" said that I had a third option: I could just end the whole thing altogether.

I was seriously considering that choice when my dad looked at me and suggested that I just try it for another week. If things didn't work out, I could come home. Knowing that I didn't need to make an immediate choice kept me from despair. I had a little more time to figure things out without losing too much in the meantime. I decided that I would take the opportunity that my dad had given me and prove to everyone the kind of person and teammate I really was. I would not let Joe or "the beast" win.

When I headed back to campus, I had no idea how great the battle would be and that I would eventually surrender. It was a spiritual battle like I had never faced before. The Dean of Men disagreed with the president's decision regarding my reinstatement and decided that in order to get my eligibility back, I had to meet with Joe and have devotions with him during quiet time on a daily basis. I knew that as a Christian I should forgive Joe, but I just couldn't do it. I felt that the Dean of Men was setting me up for failure, and I couldn't handle any more of that. I also knew that if I didn't get myself out of the situation, "the beast" would lead me to do something from which there would be no return.

The following Tuesday, I packed up my car and headed for home. I cried the entire fourteen-hour trip, listened to music and prayed constantly. Once I arrived at my front door, I collapsed in my parents' arms. No words were spoken, but we all knew that it was time to pick up the pieces and start in a different direction.

Chapter 4 –
You Can't Make
This Stuff Up

After I was home from college for a few days, my mom suggested that I get a job. The only job readily available was on a road construction crew. I knew nothing about road construction, found it to be very monotonous, and hated every minute of my time on the job! Because of my lack of talent in pouring and smoothing concrete, I was laughed at, ridiculed, and sworn at by others on the crew. I lasted about three weeks on the job and I quit after purposely tipping over a port-a-potty which was in use by another crew member.

Fortunately, my uncle offered me a job helping him out on the family farm. I had always enjoyed being around my uncle and knew that working with him would be fun. We had lots of good talks about my situation, and I appreciated that he didn't judge me for leaving school, and he helped me through my depression about not being enrolled in a basketball program for the fall.

During that time I was looking at other colleges and tried out at another Midwestern school. I had a good tryout and scrimmage in front of the coach and athletic director. Afterwards they offered me a scholarship for the spring semester. I accepted their offer and felt that I was on my way to getting over the disaster of the previous year.

Due to transfer regulations, I had to sit out a year but was able to practice with the team and get to know the players. A key player on the team became my best friend, and we spent much time together talking about nothing but basketball. It wasn't long before I became one of the guys and began to be well known around campus. Even though I wasn't playing, my practices were good, and I felt confident that the next year, when I would actually be on the team, would be a good year. In the meantime, I worked on my game and found that it was improving.

The following fall I played in my first game in over a year, and I was pumped for it. I didn't play as well as I had planned but managed to score a respectable sixteen points. As the season progressed, things improved for me and the team. We developed a rhythm, and by Christmas break we were contenders. Unfortunately, things went bad during break: two starters were suspended for stealing, and my best friend on the team was sidelined for academic issues. Our point guard and I were the only starters coming back from break, but I felt that we could handle the job, at least until the coach decided to bench me and play some of the other guys in order to give them some experience. I was shattered by that decision and found myself not wanting to play anymore. For the first time in my life, basketball became something that I dreaded. The "beast" had left me alone for a while, but I began to feel his presence once again.

Although I had been playing in some games, I was frustrated because the coach kept taking me out, and in one game when I was taking a steal in for a layup, my leg buckled, and I fell to the ground. I think my ego was more injured than my leg was, but because of my embarrassment I screamed in pain. After a few tests the trainers determined that I had merely strained my ACL and hadn't suffered any serious injury. I milked the pain for a few weeks because I just didn't want to play. However, by the time tournament rolled around, I had a change of heart and decided to give it my best. We were up against the top seed in the first round, and I played hard. It was a great game, but we came up short, and the bitter season ended for me and the team.

I didn't know it at the time, but my coach from my previous college had attended the tournament, and we met after the game. We had a nice visit, during which I told him that I missed playing for him. He said that he would be happy to have me come back to play for him but that it had to be my decision with no pressure from him. I told him that I would think it over and be in touch.

When I told my parents about our talk, they were hesitant about my returning to an environment that had caused so much pain. It was a letter from the new Dean of Men at my former school stating that I could come back with a fresh start and no hard feelings that changed their minds. We took this letter as an answer to prayer, and I knew that I needed to return to finish my college basketball career. I had peace of mind about this decision and was then able to focus on another matter that had been bothering me.

During Christmas I had starting seeing the sister of one of my best friends. We spent time together for a few weeks over Christmas, but she attended college in Florida, so when she had to return to school after break, our relationship became a long-distance one. We had a hard time being apart for five months, so I was looking forward to the summer when we could see each other more often. I had a lot to make up for because I had not always treated her very well when we were together. Because of that, she was cautious and didn't want to fully commit to the relationship. I couldn't blame her because I had a knack for ruining relationships and putting pressure where there didn't need to be any. Despite many setbacks, time together and apart, we managed to have a good summer and decided that when she returned to school to finish her senior year and I returned to my first school as a junior that we would not let our being apart ruin our relationship.

Once back on campus at my first college, I had to deal with mixed emotions. On the one hand, I was grateful for the opportunity to come back and play for a team that I loved. On the other hand, I was petrified of what people would think of me based on the decision I had made a couple years earlier. "The beast" was once again making me question my abilities, decisions, and self-worth.

The first couple of months were tough, but old and new friends helped me get through, and in the beginning, my girlfriend was supportive of my decision to return to my first college. However, the distance between our schools started to wear on our relationship. I visited her when I could and really didn't mind the six-hour drive because it gave me time to think about our situation and how we were going to make it work. I was hoping to be engaged after she graduated at the end of the school year, but I still had another year ahead of me. I avoided worrying about what we were going to do by concentrating on basketball.

It was an incredible season for me and the team. Our team was stacked with talent; we were ranked in the top ten for most of the season; and I was averaging twelve points per game. Qualifying for the National Tournament made me realize that returning to this particular college and team was the right decision. The elation didn't last long because we came out cold and had dug ourselves into a hole by halftime. I played in the second half and helped cut their lead to just a few points, but at one point while I was streaking down the floor to the basket, the defender behind me took me out. My head hit the floor, and I was out cold. The next thing I remember is waking to learn that I had suffered a Grade II concussion and that we had lost the game by five points. I was devastated: another season over and still no national championship.

I turned my attention to my relationship with my girlfriend. To make some money for the engagement ring that I hoped to present to her at her graduation, I worked thirty to forty hours a week and saved almost every dollar I earned. Naturally I was nervous about the commitment I was about to make, but was thrilled when, with her father's blessings, we became engaged. Then because I still had at least another year of school before we could get married, I headed home to a job with a building construction company that my parents had lined up for me.

I was as unqualified for this job as I had been with the road crew, and it wasn't long before I was ready to quit. The job was grueling, and I hated being away from my girlfriend. It was also during this time that "the beast" began to emerge from wherever he had been hibernating. I was very confused about my life, my decisions, and my future. I started to question everyone and everything. I was anxious to the point of being catatonic. Sometimes when I was working on roofs several stories high, I had to pray that I would not fall while "the beast" was prodding me to simply let go and end it all.

I went on vacation with my family hoping that I could get some clarity and relief from my confusion only to fight with my parents the entire trip. When we returned home from a conversation-less nine-hour drive, I slammed the door to my room and waited until everyone was asleep to pack my bags and drive another several hours to my girlfriend's family's home. I stayed with them for a couple of weeks, worked for her father shingling roofs, and then spent some time on campus helping with summer camps. When I returned from the summer camps, my girlfriend and I fought constantly until she finally asked me to leave.

I left in the same way that I had left my family earlier in the summer and in the same way I had left two colleges and two basketball teams. I was running from my problems and "the beast" was chasing me wherever I ran. I drove into the country and spent time by a river trying to face my demons while depression began to overwhelm me. I had no idea what to do, but sometime during the night, I decided that I wanted to reconcile with my girlfriend and try to get my life back in order.

On my way back to her home, I ran into another kind of nightmare. Through some hurried and dangerous driving, I aroused the ire of another driver who decided to confront me on a gravel road that I had taken hoping to save some time.

I was riled enough about my whole situation and frantic enough about getting back to my girlfriend that I, too, was ready for a fight, and I got exactly what I wanted. Instead of facing one angry driver, I was facing three guys out to teach me a lesson.

This time I let "the beast" have his way and managed some good hits to the leader's face, punching him hard enough to break his nose. The other two, however, were more than I could handle, so when one pinned my arms behind my back, the other took shots at my ribs and face. They were relentless, but as the one holding me down tried to get a better grip, I was able to pull away, flip him over onto the ground, and the fall knocked the breath out of him. I then grabbed the third guy and started to punch him until he was almost unconscious. I did not comprehend the power of my anger and my almost superhuman strength, or maybe all three had just tired of the fight. Whatever the reason, I was the one left standing. I then grabbed their car keys from the ignition, gave them a wild throw into the cornfield, got into my car, and headed to my destination.

When I arrived at my girlfriend's house, I was a mess. My eye was swollen, and blood was dripping down my face. My ribs were so bruised that I could hardly breathe. I was just lucky that I was not lying dead alongside of a road. More than being worried about my physical condition, I was terrified by the rage that had caused me to attack people I had never met. I was horrified by my loss of control and thought that maybe I had actually turned into "the beast" himself. I only knew that I was alive because of God's protection and grace and that I needed to ask the forgiveness of my family before I could make sense of my life. My girlfriend and I patched up some things, and I headed back to Iowa to face whatever consequences I would find.

I have a loving, forgiving, and godly family who understand God's grace and are obedient to Him. Because they are who they are, they welcomed home their "prodigal" son, listened to my pain, struggled with my actions, and prayed with and for me as I got ready to return to school in the fall.

I was the only returning senior and welcomed the challenge of leading the team. I had attended a two-week revival meeting before the season began, and after seeing and feeling the Holy Spirit's presence, I made a decision to be not only a better athletic leader but also a better spiritual leader. I worked and prayed hard to put "the beast" and the past behind me. I felt good about myself, my relationship with my girlfriend, and my season. I was on a high like I was at the beginning of every season; I should have been prepared for the fall. I should have recognized the cycle of my disease even if I couldn't identify it by name.

The cycle always starts with good practices, high hopes for tournament play, some good and even great games, and good feelings about personal relationships. I was always in good standings with my teammates, was respected by the coaches, and admired by the fans. Then the bottom would fall out: I'd lose all confidence in myself and my abilities; I'd find myself crying in my room for no apparent reason; I'd find myself frustrated about my relationship with my girlfriend, friends, teammates. This is the cycle that everyone with bi-polar disease goes through. I just didn't know that I had it at the time, and not knowing why I was experiencing these up and down feelings made the situation even worse.

This latest cycle involved two breakups with my girlfriend, who by then had become my fiancé, a major screaming and yelling match with my teammates in the locker room during an important game, and the end of another season without a championship. I was so depressed that I contemplated suicide for a second time, and it was only by God's grace that I did not follow through and was able to once again plow through the depression to the other side.

After the final season of my senior year, I concentrated on my classes and somehow managed to graduate *Summa Cum Laude.* The fact that I had completed one of my goals of attending college was a big relief to both me and my parents, and I looked forward to trying out for an international team where, if I couldn't play for the NBA, at least I would be playing basketball somewhere.

The tryout was grueling: we conditioned for over an hour without even touching a basketball. There were about one hundred and fifty players trying out in the beginning, but many didn't make it through the conditioning and others simply quit. The competition among those who remained was intense. Because it was a tryout, there was no team play and everyone was naturally out to prove himself better than the others. In the end, I was told that I would be able to play on a team in the Philippines, but I was concerned about the political unrest there and decided to wait until the next tryout which would not be until the spring.

Since I had no other plans until the next tryout, I decided to enroll in graduate school and took a full load of classes to make up some teaching credits that I was lacking. To make some much needed money, I worked delivering pizzas and coached middle school soccer and JV boys basketball at my old high school.

I was so busy that the fall and first semester of grad school seemed to fly by. I enjoyed coaching soccer and learned from the experience that if I weren't able to play basketball, I might be a good coach. It was during Christmas break that my future in playing basketball was determined for me by an unfortunate accident during a pick-up game with some high school friends.

The game brought back many great memories, and we fell into a routine of playing together like we had in high school. Towards the end of the game, I stole the ball, and just as I went in for a layup, I felt something in my leg snap. Because of the extreme pain, I was sure that it was more serious than a broken bone. The x-ray at the hospital showed that I had torn my Achilles tendon, and the doctor told me that it would be at least nine months before I could even consider running again. There was no guarantee that I would make a full recovery, and I certainly would not be making the spring tryout for the international team.

A few days after the accident, I had reconstructive surgery on my Achilles tendon. The surgery went well, but I had to wear a cast for a month and then a walking cast for six weeks. While I was wearing the walking cast, the doctor removed an insert every two weeks to stretch the tendon. I was in terrible pain throughout the ordeal, and my emotional state was no better. The only thing that kept me going was coaching the JV basketball team.

Coaching came easily to me, and I began to think that I had found my calling. I understood the way to motivate the young men because I knew what it took for me to stay motivated. I became so wrapped up in the coaching that I almost forgot about my injury. We had a winning season because of the hard work from the team, and I was very proud of their accomplishments. Within nine months, I was not only coaching a basketball team but also playing in a men's basketball league. I had found a new passion and a new dream. I was going to be a coach.

Chapter 5 –
Third Time's a Charm

I was still delivering pizza and coaching during the fall of my last year in grad school, but the work load was starting to wear me down, and I was starting to withdraw from my family and friends. There was a void in my life that dating, coaching, family, friends, and activity could not fill. I was very angry at God for taking away my basketball dreams, and I started smoking and drinking here and there to relieve some stress. I was doing anything to make me happy, and nothing did. I hated myself on every level and hated what I was becoming.

One night, however, things began to look a little brighter. My parents and I attended a performance of *The Sound of Music* at my sister's college, and I was immediately attracted to a young lady who was in the production. After the performance I asked my sister to introduce me to her, but at the time only managed to get her e-mail address. We started corresponding, and her emails gave me something to look forward to each day. From emails we moved to phone calls and finally met each other that Thanksgiving when she came home with my sister for the holiday. I think I fell in love at first sight, and we had many things in common, not the least of which was that we had both been engaged twice before and had broken it off. Four months later her father gave me his permission to marry Alicia, and by August of that year, we were married.

I got my first teaching and coaching job at two schools in northern Minnesota, and while Alicia was finishing up classes at her college in the Twin Cities, we lived solely on my salary. We lived with Alicia's parents for about a month and then moved into a basement apartment which wasn't much, but it was our "first home."

Marriage brought with it a whole new set of anxieties, and it wasn't long before I wasn't sure that I enjoyed being married. Some of the same old emotions began to show themselves, and I had difficulty communicating with Alicia about them for fear that she would think I was crazy like so many others had thought before. And like before I began to close myself off from her and started living a life that was foreign to both her and my family.

I had periods where I went without sleeping, and when I did, it was after I had had several beers and fell asleep on the couch. The marriage made me feel claustrophobic; I was severely depressed, and our marriage was in serious jeopardy.

I was doing my best to push Alicia away and make her feel as though she was the problem in the relationship. I was a master manipulator, and there were many nights she would go to bed believing my lies. I was verbally abusive and "the beast" came up with new ways each day to push her further and further away. I began smoking more and the occasional drink was becoming a weekend marathon. I felt that God had tricked me into marriage, and I blamed Him for the mess I was in.

Alicia was the strong one in our marriage, and she loved me too much to just give up. She kept praying for me and believing in me despite the hurt I was causing her, and although there were some good moments, the damage created by my manic depression was almost too much for her to bear. The bottom fell out when our landlady decided to kick us out of the basement and we had to move back in with Alicia's parents. This made matters even worse because just when I needed most to be alone, I lost any privacy that the basement even slightly afforded. And then I was relieved of my duties as the math teacher at one of my schools because I was only certified in physical education and should not have been teaching math. By God's grace we finished the school year and made it to the summer break with our marriage still intact.

We spent the summer working at a golf resort, applying for teaching jobs all over Iowa and Minnesota, and even signing up online for jobs anywhere in the U.S. We were desperate for a teaching job anywhere: the bills were piling up, and we had no steady source of income.

In late August we received a call from a school on a Navajo reservation in Arizona to teach Navajo and Hopi Indian students. The phone interview went well, and the best part was that they wanted both of us to teach at the school. If I accepted the job, the head coach said he could use me as an assistant coach and I would be the head JV coach. We were promised financial help with our moving expenses and retroactive pay since they had already started school. We were thrilled with the offer and ecstatic that we finally had a job. We really had no choice, didn't need to think it over, and even though we didn't even have time to pray about it, we thought this an answer to prayer. So with very little money in our pockets, we packed our bags and prepared for a trip across country to Arizona for the start of a new adventure, and what an adventure it was!

Chapter 6 -
The Reservation

Even on my worst days I have a pretty good sense of humor, but it wasn't until we reached my Uncle Tim's house in Mulvane, Kansas, that I found anything funny about what happened next.

Because we had little money, we couldn't afford a U-Haul or Penske truck, so my father-in-law worked out a deal to use the marching band trailer to help move our belongings to Arizona. The trailer was bigger than the suburban that we were using to haul the unit, but we still had little room to spare. Needless to say, we were both excited and nervous about the job, the trip, and the way we were going to have to maneuver the vehicles. We were thankful that my mother-in-law decided to travel with us and were relieved to have a third driver.

We were not more than ten miles down the road, when I realized that I would not be able to control the trailer if

I drove faster than 45 mph. That set me off, and I cussed up and down about there being no way we could make the trip and that we might as well forget the trip and job, stay in Minnesota, and give up on the whole deal. I didn't like hearing both Alicia and her mother tell me that we should just travel safely at whatever speed we could manage, but since we really had no other options, I climbed back into the Suburban and started out again.

I felt helpless and knew that I needed God's help to keep going, so I asked Him for patience and for help in understanding His plans for us. I knew that He always knows what is best even when we don't, and I trusted Him to use this move as a way to heal my marriage.

The normal thirteen-hour trip took us eighteen and a half nerve-wracking hours. I was in a constant state of frustration and fear as every semi that passed me caused the trailer to serve back and forth. I was never quite sure if I could keep it on the road, but we somehow managed to arrive at my uncle's house around 2:30 in the morning. The look on his face when he saw what we were intending to park in his driveway was enough to make us all break down in laughter. The trailer was so large that it cast a shadow from the street lights onto his house, and the noise of the motor caused lights to go on in the neighboring houses. My Uncle Tim always makes me laugh, and this night was no exception. As he envisioned the rest of the trip and the length of the drive we still had ahead of us,

I praised God for this comic relief. God gave me the gift of laughter to overcome my frustration, fear, and depression. I had very little sleep that night, but was able to awake the next morning to say our good-byes and to head on to Flagstaff.

We made it to Flagstaff by nightfall, got a good night's sleep, and the next morning said good-bye to my mother-in-law who was going to wait for Alicia's father to arrive from Phoenix and then follow us to the reservation to help us unpack and settle in. It was difficult to say goodbye not knowing what lay ahead, but we were determined to keep on keeping on and depending upon God to protect and guide us.

The drive to the reservation was a little over an hour from Flagstaff, and although we thought we were driving into town with our eyes wide opened, we were not prepared for what we did and didn't see. The houses were very tiny and run down, and they were situated on nothing but sand. There didn't appear to be any grass in sight, and for people from the Midwest, it was alien territory. We were thankful for a McDonald's and KFC but wondered what we would find once we arrived at the school.

The school was about a mile into town, and as shocked as we were when we drove into town, we were more shocked and pleasantly surprised to find a state-of-the art building in the midst of a desert wilderness. The people at the school were very friendly and welcoming, and we heaved a sigh of relief when we saw our single bedroom house surrounded by similar homes occupied by other teachers at the school. When Alicia's parents arrived to help us unpack, we were grateful to find the house big enough for our possessions and thankful for her parents' support even though we all had some obvious concerns. The next morning my in-laws headed back to Minnesota, and Alicia and I set out to begin our new lives, determined to make our marriage work and to prove to ourselves and others that we had made the right decision in taking this job.

Proving this was going to be difficult because we hit some major glitches right from the start. We found out that some of the promises that were made to us regarding moving expenses and retroactive pay were indeed merely promises and that there was an immense amount of paperwork to fill out before we could begin teaching; some of this was our fault because we had neglected to get any of the promises on paper before moving. As a result we had several arguments with the principal, and because we were on reservation land, we were dealing with different rules and regulations than what we were used to back home. We were facing a situation in which our hands were tied and were involved in a battle which we could not possibly win. It was very difficult to control my anger regarding the broken promises, but we had no options other than to try to make the best of the situation. So the drama quieted down, and Alicia and I began our teaching assignments: I would be teaching health and physical education in the beautiful high school, and Alicia would be teaching music in a run-down trailer.

The first few months were without incident. We spent lots of time together getting to know each other again, and things were good between us. We had to rely on each other for everything because we had no family nearby and had not made many friends. On weekends we drove to Flagstaff to eat a nice meal and do some shopping. We counted on Iowa Hawkeye football games to give us a taste of home, and our two mongrel pets, Sporty and Chauncey kept us good company. For the most part, things were good.

Unfortunately, we were still not making much money, and I started gambling on football games hoping to make enough to help us get by. I had always loved sports and knew enough about them to make money on them. That fall I made quite a bit, which helped us stay afloat, but gambling became a destructive addiction and began to consume my life. Of course, Alicia did not approve of what I was doing, but it was hard to argue about the fact that I was bringing in some much needed income, and that fact kept me addicted to gambling on sports for many years.

When basketball season started, I took over a JV program that wasn't expected to do much, but we went 14-4to win our conference. That record won me the support of the community, and when the head basketball coach decided to leave at the end of the season, I was excited about the possibility of becoming the next head coach. Alicia surprised me by her excitement over the possibility that staying another year would help us to pay off credit card debt and possibly even allow us to save for a house when we moved back to the Midwest. We missed our families and our life back home, but I had learned a lot that season, had had a great experience with the team, and we were making enough money to cover any little expense we had while living on the reservation. We had hopes that we would be able to live another year in the desert, as long as we remembered not to drink the water.

Satan and his emissary, "the beast," however, had other plans, and while they had laid relatively low during the year, they barged right in before the year ended. We were living in a culture that had spiritual beliefs very different from Christian beliefs. Their beliefs were in medicine men and spirits of the past, not in an atoning Savior and Lord, and Alicia and I felt that our ministry within this culture was important. We believed that our witness was making a difference: the community supported us, and we had the respect of our students and team. The only person who did not seem to care for us was the school principal, and we never knew the reason. His opinion, however, was so valued by the community that when I interviewed for the head coaching job, he was able to convince the hiring committee to not hire either of us for the coming year. I couldn't see how one man could have such control, and "the beast" was, once again, causing my confidence to hit rock bottom. It was the second time in as many years that I had not been rehired, and I was angry!

Alicia and my parents again calmed me down and suggested strongly that I wait patiently to see how the Lord was going to bless this situation. So, we packed up our belongings, this time in a Penske truck, and headed back to Minnesota to await the next chapter of the story.

Chapter 7 – Chapter Seven

By the end of the summer I had two job offers, one at the high school I had graduated from and one in a very small Iowa town. It was a difficult decision because my dad taught at my high school, and I knew it would be fun working with him and rebuilding a program with the support of my family and many people I had known my whole life. However, the other school offered me more money, and I felt that it was important for me to start fresh again on my own. So I took the job in the small town where I would be teacher, athletic director, and head boys basketball coach.

With the little money that Alicia and I had saved, we were able to put a down payment on a house. Alicia got a job in a nearby town, and things seemed to go along smoothly for us as we began the school year. My first basketball season went amazingly well, and we ended the season 13-9, losing in the district semi-finals to a team that went on to the final four in the state championship. I was named Coach of the Year in the conference because I had turned around a program that had been unsuccessful for over a decade. At the end of the season, we learned that Alicia was pregnant with our first child. It was a good year.

The pregnancy, however, was a different story. Due to downsizing in Alicia's company, she lost her job and her health insurance. She became severely ill with hyperemesis, an unrelenting case of morning sickness. As a result she was sick for the first seven months of her pregnancy and lost an unhealthy amount of weight. After many hospitalizations, the bills began to mount up. We consulted with a specialist in Minnesota and were able to get the situation under control. Our daughter, Jerah, was born on December 22nd. She was our perfect Christmas present.

I should have been on top of the world. I had a healthy wife, a beautiful daughter, and a good job, but, as always, basketball was my emotional barometer. We finished the second season with a disappointing 13-10 record, mainly because we never really played with the desire or passion that we had the year before. I was in severe depression, became distant in my relationship with Alicia, and left her with most of the responsibility of raising Jerah. In the meantime, Alicia had decided to go back to school, and although it was ultimately the right decision for our future, it left us with my salary as our sole source of income, and she had no health insurance. Added to the regular cost-of-living budget items were our many outstanding medical bills. We were getting further and further behind financially. We argued constantly about money and my responsibility as a husband and a man, all of which added to my depression and anger.

That summer Alicia returned to her family in Minnesota, and I went back to my parents and worked as a pizza delivery driver. We were attempting to catch-up financially any way we could, but the living arrangements created even more strain on our relationship and compounded my depression.

I started gambling again and over the summer amassed a little over six-thousand dollars. One night because I needed a large amount of money to pay some overdue credit card debt, I placed the total amount on a single baseball game and lost it all. I had been hiding my gambling from Alicia, but we were in such desperate financial straits that I knew it eventually would come out.

When we returned to our house in the fall, we had no running water. We were on well water and thought that the problem was a result of the summer drought and intense heat. Our well would sometimes fill enough to maybe do a load of laundry, but it was dry within a week. We tried to solve the problem by buying thirty gallon jugs of water to use to flush the toilets and to drink, but, of course, that was a costly solution. Alicia's parents helped us by paying a farmer to dig a trench and install a backup tank so that we would at least have water in an emergency. For two months we survived by using the shower at the school, the laundromat in town, and by filling our jugs with water at both places.

The problem was finally solved when I was in the basement one night fooling with the water softener. I noticed a lever that I had not seen before and decided to pull it since I didn't think that doing so could cause any worse problem than we already had. As soon as I did, water started rushing through the pipes! Apparently, and who knows when or how, the bypass valve had been switched and all of our well water had been running straight into the ground. Alicia was thrilled to have water, but I was furious over the wasted time, energy and money we had spent, and the humiliation we had suffered while using public facilities for our personal needs. It's a bit funny in retrospect, but was not so much at the time, just another chapter in the story.

I recovered from the experience as I always did by looking forward to the basketball season, and with a 6' 8" post player and some very good guards surrounding him, I had high hopes for this group of players. We won the first twelve games and were ranked third in the state when we were scheduled to play the number one team. We lost that game by twenty-one points, but the score was not indicative of the way we had played. I was worried about the team's reaction to the loss and was discouraged by losing the game in the fourth quarter when we had been trailing by only one point at the half.

We lost the next game, and I was falling into a state of depression and failure. However, the next six games belonged to us, and despite a close loss in the last regular season game, I began to realize that I had a pretty good team on my hands and could smell a state tournament berth. We finished the regular season with an 18-3 record, the best in school history, and I was riding high! We breezed through our district to the district championship title winning by an average of twenty-three and a half points per game. I went into the sub-state final believing that God was going to bless me with a state tournament berth.

I prepared the team for the next game the best I knew how, but I had not prepared myself for a possible loss. So when we lost the game as a result of a very controversial three-point call, I was barely able to shake hands with opposing team, let alone congratulate them on the win. "The beast" was ready to devour everything in sight, and I held on to this loss for a very long time.

That loss ended the season and almost ended my marriage. I was in deep emotional trouble, loathing everything about myself and wallowing in self-pity. Our financial situation was disastrous, and my relationship with my wife was even worse. I separated myself from everyone and everything I loved. I became a chain smoker and started to use alcohol as an escape from my problems. I had spent the past summer away from my family delivering pizzas and working at summer camps for naught; we were no closer to digging ourselves out of the financial mess we were in. My thirty-thousand dollar salary didn't come close to covering daily needs, astronomical medical bills, and unavoidable credit card debt. I had tried to work with a company to consolidate our debt and lessen the burden of high interest payments, but the company randomly chose which bill to pay and how much money to withdraw per payment. Since I was not in control of those payments, I was frequently overdrawn and piling up more debt to the bank. I had run out of possible solutions, I was convinced we had hit rock bottom. HA!

While Alicia and I were doing dishes one night, the county sheriff arrived to hand us paperwork for a lawsuit being filed against us by one of our credit card companies. I finally had to tell Alicia everything about our finances and in tears had to tell her that we had no other choice but to declare bankruptcy. Because Alicia is who she is, rather than screaming at me and accusing me of ruining our lives, she simply questioned where we had gone wrong. The one blessing remaining to me was a wife who loved me in spite of the mess I had made of everything.

Alicia's father went with us to Des Moines to file for bankruptcy. It took well over an hour for the lawyer to go through all of our bills, debts, and assets, and for us to arrive at an agreement about what we could and could not keep: we would lose our house but keep our car. As Alicia welled up with tears, the lawyer told us that bankruptcy was meant for people like us who found themselves in very unfortunate circumstances and told us to think of it as a fresh start. My life had been a life of fresh starts and second chances, and I was thankful for another one: a fresh start with my finances, and more importantly, a second chance with my family.

Chapter 8 – All Things Work Together for Good

Nothing remains quiet or hidden in any small town. After being humiliated by the bankruptcy and losing our house, I was further humiliated when a few of my students saw me using government assistance checks, to buy milk for Jerah, at a local grocery. As a result, I didn't feel like staying on in my teaching job at the high school and started applying for teaching jobs elsewhere. I was blessed to be hired as a physical education teacher and head basketball coach in another town in Iowa. It was far enough away that I had never been in that conference as a player or a coach, and far enough away from friends and family that no one knew of our past financial woes. It looked like I would truly be able to start with a clean slate, and I looked forward to putting the "beast" and my problems behind me ---- once again!

And once again, the move was not without a major setback and some comic relief. Because we had left our house and had nowhere to live, we stored all of our belongings in a rental unit near my parents' house. We were in a hurry when we moved and probably didn't do a very good job of searching for reputable storage facilities, so we should not have been surprised about the condition of our things when we arrived to retrieve them. Nevertheless, we were shocked to find that everything we owned had been damaged by water and that mold had begun to take over. The rental facility refused to take responsibility for the damaged items, and the only things we managed to salvage were those items stored in plastic totes or ones stacked well off the floor. This time Alicia did not remain her usual calm self. Instead she piled all of our damaged items on the front step of the rental office and wrote a sarcastic note thanking them for "allowing us to pay for our ruined storage unit and destroyed possessions." By this time I was so overwhelmed by everything that had gone wrong since our wedding day, I simply laughed, shrugged my shoulders, and thought "bring on the next disaster." I didn't think it could be worse than anything we had already faced.

Our new job and new home was anything but a disaster; it was another blessing from God. Even with our credit history, we were able to rent the apartment we wanted and were delighted when my future team arrived to help us unload the truck. I felt that this town was meant for us as educators and parents. Alicia had received her teaching certificate before leaving our previous home and also would be teaching in the school system. We now had two bread earners in the family and thought that maybe we could even begin saving some money to use to replace the house we had lost.

Unfortunately, the one thing that I did not leave behind in the move was my gambling addiction and my belief that I should be able to provide more for my family than just paying the day-to-day bills. I believed that I was knowledgeable enough about sports and that I had developed enough shrewd gambling skills to be as successful in my bets as I had been in Arizona. I spent much time researching and watching games rather than spending time with my family, and I was not enjoying myself. I knew that something was very wrong with me. I was not finding happiness with my family, and gambling was not satisfying the void that was growing inside me. "The beast" was growling loudly and strongly, and I couldn't resist him even with prayer. I was not sleeping and was physically and emotionally in turmoil and exhaustion. Alicia was very worried about me, but neither of us talked about the situation. The only thing that stopped the gambling was that I had to start concentrating on basketball because the season was ready to start.

My basketball situation was much different from the ones I had come into in my other coaching jobs. Rather than trying to build a team out of nothing, I would be coaching a team that had played in the state tournament the year before. Many of the seniors on that team had graduated, but there was a great core of younger players who were returning. I viewed this first season as a learning one and an important one in terms of recruiting and growth.

The season was a roller coaster ride which ended prematurely in the first round of districts and with a record of 11-9. Despite the support of the community and what many considered a season of accomplishments, I was frustrated, depressed and didn't want to take it out on my family. Rather than returning home, I took long drives to clear my head, but doing that caused me to miss out on Jerah's life, and she was growing up quickly. She was not the only one I had been ignoring due to my obsession with basketball. I had been ignoring my Christian walk, and I was extremely uncomfortable with the witness I was presenting. Very few would look at me and see me as the born-again Christian that I professed to be.

I didn't deal with either of these issues at the time. Instead I focused on taking my team to various summer camps and getting them ready for the next season. It was a season that provided many learning experiences, many controversial calls and technical fouls, some errors by the officials, and I left many games feeling that we had gotten the short end of the stick. However, through a great effort by the team and coaches and by rebounding from disappointing calls and plays, we ended the regular season sixteen and three, ready to head to post-season play.

I had never given up my dream of winning a state championship, and again I believed this would be the year. We worked very hard to win some hard fought district games, one against a team coached by the man who had preceded me and had taken my current team to the state tournament. Our hard work and my determination to be the best coach I could be helped us clinch the district championship.

We had some very difficult district games. We were often the underdogs, had to change some of our playing strategy, and, because of our opponents' talents, faced the need to play nearly flawless games. I can proudly say that we survived all of the challenges and made it to the final sub-state game. In the end this was the game that I had been preparing for and dreaming of for many, many years, and it did not disappoint me. There was extreme amount of tension throughout the game, but my team went to the floor with ferocious determination and scored a 70-52 victory at the buzzer.

The student body erupted and stormed the court as I tried to fight my way through the crowd to shake the hands of our opponents. I cannot even begin to describe my excitement or the silliness of the smile on my face when the athletic director of the host school offered to get a ladder and scissors so that we could cut down the net as a symbol of our victory. After my post season interview with the radio announcer, I joined the team on the court to cut the final piece of netting. My celebration was further enhanced when I saw that many of my aunts, uncles, and cousins had attended the game and were cheering as loudly as anyone in the gym. The crowning glory was being hugged by my wife who was eight months pregnant with our second child. For that moment I was at peace. I was satisfied with myself as a coach. I was finally living the dream. I was going to coach in the place where my dream had begun many years earlier, the Wells Fargo Arena. I would be part of one of the teams contending for the Iowa State Boys Basketball Championship.

I entered the week prior to the state tournament enjoying the pomp and circumstance that comes with being a championship contender and thanking God for His many blessings. For that brief week, the world was our playground, and we were treated like royalty. The whole experience was second to none, exactly as I dreamed it would be, and was not diminished by our sixty eight to fifty one first round loss. I was never more proud of my team of players and thanked them for the best year of my basketball life. We may not have been state champions but we were champions in every sense of the word.

Chapter 9 –
"The Beast"
Gets a Name

April was always a bad month for me as far as my depression was concerned, and the April after the state tournament was no different. Once the excitement of tournament ended, I tried to focus on my new baby girl, but memories of the kind of dad I was when Jerah was a baby kept me from becoming too attached to Sophie. I handled the anxiety of fatherhood in the same way that I had handled it before and spent my time on long drives just so that I didn't have to be at home where the pressure and anxiety was at its worst. My relationship with Alicia was deteriorating because she couldn't understand why being at home with my family didn't make me happy and why I was always so angry with them.

I knew that something was very wrong with me but didn't know what to do about it. I wasn't able to pray because of the guilt that I was feeling over the sin in my life, and I didn't want to talk to anyone about it, especially my family. In the process all I did was lash out at Alicia and say very hurtful things.

It came to a point that my sister was so concerned about me that one night while she was at our home, she called my dad. Both he and my mother had been consulting with a family friend, Dr. Marv, who was experienced in treating bipolar disorder and its treatment. So when my parents turned up at our home that night, dad had a name for "the beast." He also said that he and my mom would help me conquer my disease in any way they could. Dad, Mom, Alicia and I determined that maybe Alicia should spend the summer with her parents in Minnesota while recovering from her pregnancy and that I should spend the summer with them where I could meet with the therapist.

During that summer I spent every other week in therapy and was on Abilify and Lamictal for medical treatment. The medicine was very effective, and I began to feel that I was getting a bit of control over my emotions. One negative side effect of the medicine was that I wanted to sleep all of the time, which, of course, did not help because once Alicia returned home, she interpreted my lethargy as another way of avoiding any interaction with her or the girls. Fortunately, through some of the therapy that we had as a couple, Alicia began to understand my bipolar disorder and continued to work on our marriage with me. I praised God daily for blessing me with this diagnosis and for giving my family back to me. I thanked Him for the ability to hold my children without feeling that they were smothering me and for the ability to see my responsibility to them as a blessing.

We are warned in Scripture that Satan attacks most ferociously when we are in closest relationship with God. Satan doesn't want us to praise or worship God, so he tempts us when we are most confident in our own strength, which I was because of the success of the medicine and therapy, or in an area where we are most vulnerable, which for me had always been basketball. That year's season was the perfect target.

We started the season 16-1 and were ranked in the top ten in the state, but ended the season playing our worst basketball of the year. The season abruptly ended in the first round of district play as we lost three of our last four basketball games. As always, I had thought that success in basketball would bring success in other areas of my life, so I had concentrated on tournament play even though Alicia had left me to go back to her parents in Minnesota. To add to the frustration, the school where I was teaching was consolidating their athletic programs with another school in the area, and although I had been given the head coaching job, there was talk of their cutting my teaching position. I would never be able to support a family of four on my coaching salary alone.

It seemed as though nothing was working out in my life: my basketball coaching career was headed in the wrong direction, my wife and I were talking more and more about divorce, my panic attacks and uncontrollable outbursts at Alicia were multiplying, and the medication and therapy for my bipolar disorder were seeming to be a waste of time and money.

After talking to my therapist, I started on a different medication and felt that I was coping well enough to try again to work things out with Alicia. Unsure of her reaction, I headed up to Minnesota and was both surprised and grateful when she, too, wanted to try again. We had a wonderful weekend together with the girls, and I began to realize that I could not count on medication alone to solve all of my problems. I knew that I needed to monitor myself more closely. I may not have been responsible for my disease, but I could be responsible for monitoring my thoughts and behaviors as I learned more and more about being a person with bipolar disorder and as I began to accept that it would always be a part of my life.

As predicted, I was laid off from my teaching job and again had to look for a job for myself and a home for my family. This move was particularly hard because we liked the community we were living in and had actually saved some money to maybe buy a house in town. I started searching late in the spring and was fortunate to sign a contract with a 4A school only an hour's drive from my hometown and closer to Alicia's parents' home than we had been for a number of years. It seemed to be a good move, especially when arriving at our new home, we found the basketball team and their families waiting to help us move in. Sadly, that would be the last goodwill gesture this "home" had to offer. We soon found ourselves a round peg in a square hole.

Teaching was fine for me, but for Alicia it was a nightmare. Almost from the beginning she was so harassed and bullied by the administration at her school that she was begging to quit after just a few months into the academic year. I was frustrated with her distress because I was trying to find a light at the end of the tunnel by focusing on the upcoming basketball season. However, the 'beast" took full advantage of my frustration and her distress during an intense argument, which resulted in my leaving home and heading toward the casino where I could just be a guy with no problems out for a good time rather than a guy with bipolar disorder, an unhappy wife, and a family I had to support. I won hundreds of dollars that night, but I didn't feel any better when I returned home, and an addiction that I thought I had conquered grabbed hold of me again. It is an addiction that I struggle with even today.

Once basketball season started, my life became the same type of hell that Alicia had been living in. Alicia's battle was with her administration; mine was with my coaching staff. I worked hard to build my program, but my coaching staff seemed to be undermining every effort. I tried to relate to them by spending time with them outside of practice to show them that we were together in our goals for the team, but the "camaraderie" only enhanced my struggle with alcohol and did nothing to appease their bitterness and animosity towards me. The reason for the mutiny that eventually ensued, I figured out later, was that two of the coaches on my staff had interviewed for the same head coaching position and were naturally bitter and angry that someone from outside had gotten the job. Our 4-17 record was a perfect picture of a disastrous year for both Alicia and me.

In the beginning I was thrilled to be coaching in a larger school in a larger conference, but I quickly learned that bigger is not always better and found myself wishing that I had stayed put in the lovely little town where Alicia and I felt comfortable, liked, and accepted, a place where we could raise our children. I had been receiving calls from staff and parents at my previous school asking whether I would return if a teaching and coaching position opened up. So when I had to make a decision about firing my entire coaching staff or resigning my job and moving once again, the decision wasn't difficult.

The decision, however, was not without reaction from the community. I was ripped to shreds by the media who questioned my leaving after only one season and then concluded that I was not the right hire from the beginning.

The "beast" was in full attack, causing me to doubt myself in every way and throwing all of the community criticism up in my face. The only thing that kept me going was the thought of returning "home."

As excited as we were about the move, we were concerned about where we would live. We had a growing family and did not want to rent, but didn't know if we could handle two mortgages. The owners of a house we were looking at dropped the price to something we felt we could afford, and we thanked God for another answer to prayer. We used some of our savings for the down payment and for improvements we needed to make on the house. The remainder was to help maintain the two mortgages, and we were confident that we would be free of one before too long.

Although there were a few questioning our return, for the most part we were welcomed back with open arms. Alicia liked her new job, and basketball went smoothly. We exceeded expectations by ending the season 13-7. The "beast" seemed to be under control with just a few minor flare ups which we managed to handle together. We seemed to finally be on the right track.

That was until February, when it was becoming increasingly difficult to make two house payments. Once again I turned to smoking and gambling to escape and to solve financial problems. Thanks to Alicia's help and prayers, I didn't sink to previous lows and managed to think more rationally about our situation.

Like many in this economic downturn and housing crisis, I turned to the bank for help with the mortgage on the house I was trying to sell. I told them that I needed to skip the next month's payment, but they told me that they could not help me until I was three month's delinquent. I had tried to do the ethical thing, but when I was turned down, I played the system, skipped the next three months, and waited for the bank's next move.

By this time we were out of money and options as far as our housing situation was concerned. We had to get rid of the house we were no longer living in and started the process of a short sale, a process which led to more frustration, anger, impatience, and lasted more than a year. During that time we lost many offers on the house and learned that the house had mold in the basement. We are now probably facing foreclosure on that house because of the mold and because we have no resources to fix the problem.

Adding to the frustration over the house was a disappointing basketball season. We ended the season 7-15, the worst of my career at this school. I felt as though I was bottoming out and had no where to turn. It was while listening to a sermon about the way we are viewed in our own town that finally put everything into a Godly perspective for me.

I had taken a long time, but I began to realize that I had always been concerned about what people thought of me as a performer or coach rather than what God thought of me as a person. I was concerned that my friends thought I was fun to be around rather than being concerned about my sinfulness in God's eyes. I was concerned about winning at the gambling table rather than being concerned about being the husband and father that my family deserved. It is easy for me to blame my condition on my bipolar disorder and the "beast," but I have finally come to realize that as long as I want to be the one in control, I will always be disappointed in the outcome. I will never be good enough to satisfy my expectations.

God would prove himself to me again as our three year old daughter, Sophie, had a terrible accident while shopping one Sunday afternoon. She had fallen out of a shopping cart and cracked the back of her skull. We did not know it at the time but she was slowly slipping through our fingers. Upon realizing that her condition was becoming very serious, we rushed her to the hospital and pleaded with them to help our precious daughter. After a few tests they concluded she had some internal bleeding and needed to life-flight her by helicopter to the Children's Hospital in Omaha.

I drove home with Jerah and frantically began packing our things. Jerah held up one of Sophie's stuffed animals looking up at me with tears in her eyes. I immediately lost it and began sobbing in Jerah's arms. The "beast" was warring inside of me on whether to trust God in this situation or to be angry with Him. I was really struggling trying to trust God but I knew I had no other option. God had blessed me with my family and if He wanted to take one home it was ultimately His choice. I wrestled with that thought process throughout our entire two hour trip to Omaha.

I turned a two hour drive into about a ninety-minute trip caring less if an officer of the law was about to stop me. The air ambulance medical team sent us pictures via text messages of Sophie and updates on how she was doing. For the time being, that seemed to keep my wife and me calm. My wife also sensed God's presence throughout the entire trip but I was more concerned with getting to the hospital in record time.

Once we arrived at the hospital we ran up to where our little girl was resting. She was in a caged bed looking very puzzled as we came in to see her. Her pale confused face seemed to stare at us in the eyes as if she was going to be fine. It sounds crazy but it was as if she knew better than we did that things were going to work out for the best.

The doctor came in and told us that she had some bleeding in the back of her head and they were going to monitor it closely throughout the night as it had not yet reached any brain tissue. My parents left immediately upon hearing that Sophie had been in an accident, and Alicia's family, who had been with us that weekend, turned around and made the trip to Omaha. A lady from our church was already at the hospital when we arrived and was praying with us in Sophie's hospital room. We circled the bed and prayed for her many times that night once family arrived.

Alicia and I couldn't sleep as we watched our little girl rest during the long waning hours of the night. Once morning arrived they were going to take Sophie and run her through a CAT scan. We were hoping for the best but expecting the worst. The first CAT scan that they had done at the emergency room found Sophie screaming with Alicia being unable to comfort her. Naturally when they wanted to do another CAT scan here we were very unsure of how Sophie would respond. However, Sophie promised that if her Nana could go with her she would not need to be sedated. She handled this CAT scan like a champion and laid perfectly still for the doctors.

It seemed like hours had passed since the completion of the CAT scan and we were waiting to hear back from the results. Once the doctor finally came into the room he informed us that there were no signs of bleeding anywhere. It was a miracle! The "beast" had tried to convince me that God was abandoning me and that I should not put my trust in Him. God proved to be much bigger and once again showed me that He is completely in control. Our daughter was healed and tears of joy overcame my face.

God had once again brought us to our knees. Two houses lost in seven years, several jobs in the same amount of time, a marriage often in turmoil, and a future that appears doomed has brought us to our knees. How fortunate we are to be on our knees! It is the only position in which we are humble enough to know that we cannot do anything in and of ourselves. No matter how much our family and friends love us, they cannot solve our problems. We are on our own until we acknowledge that the only place where we can find strength, purpose, comfort, guidance, acceptance, courage, and hope is at the throne of God's grace.

Alicia taught me this important lesson during an in depth discussion about my salvation. She questioned me about the way I had been living and about what was really important in my life. She challenged me to make a choice about what I wanted for the rest of my life, about the kind person, husband, and father I wanted to be for Alicia and our children, about the kind of son and brother I wanted to be to my parents and sister. We had never honestly talked about this before, probably because I had never been willing to listen. She was challenging me to come "home," to my wife, my family, myself, and my God.

With God's help and my family's love, I am working to do exactly that. I have turned the house situation over to God's control; I am working at changing my behavior, speech, and attitude around my friends; I am trying to stop blaming the "beast" and my bipolar disorder for my problems; I am waking each morning striving to "die daily" to the temptations of the world; I am dedicating myself to being the spiritual leader that my family deserves. I was brought up in God's word; I am now striving to live according to it, and I am beginning to see the fruits of God's grace.

In June of 2011, our third daughter, Lucianne, was born. I am now in a place mentally and emotionally to help Alicia with our girls. It is a joy to be a father to them and a sorrow that I wasn't more of a presence when Jerah and Sophie were babies. I am so thankful that they have no recollection of the mess I was early in their lives and that Lucianne will never know that turmoil. They only know me for the father I am today. They don't care or worry about my bipolar disorder, and they love their daddy dearly.

Today Alicia and I are at peace with each other and with where we live and work. Our girls are a joy and complete our lives. God has brought me full circle, and my passion is to worship and honor Him in every area of my life. My marriage is better than it has ever been, and our relationship is healthy and loving. We have our ups and down like other married couples, but we are able to communicate with each other much more easily, and I feel confident that Alicia is not judging me when I tell her exactly the way I am feeling at any given moment. We have precious moments of praying together and sharing

Scripture. I am learning to live with my disorder, and although the "beast" occasionally rears his ugly head, his roar is less loud and his bite is less damaging. Through it all, God has remained faithful. He gives strength for each day and bright hope for each tomorrow. To God be the Glory!

Chapter 10 –
Keeping on...

Alicia and I have learned so much about living with bipolar disorder. We have learned to cope with the stigma attached to mental illness, to confess sin and to accept God's forgiveness and the forgiveness of our families and friends whom we have hurt and disappointed through the struggle, and to develop strategies that ease our anxieties, help us find solutions to problems, overcome our feelings of inadequacy, and give us a sense of belonging and normalcy. Each strategy is grounded in Scripture, and we pray that in listing them here, they might be of some help to people searching for a way to tame and conquer their own bipolar "beast."

1. **Admit that you need help** - Psalm 46:1 " God is our refuge and strength an ever-present help in trouble."

In my struggle with my bipolar disease, I had to come to a place where I called out for help. I knew that I couldn't do it on my own because I had tried many times. I felt that my sin was too great to call upon a Holy God, and, as is typical with men, my ego was too big to seek help from others. Women by nature are a bit more inclined to talk to others about their feelings, but their fear of rejection and ridicule is no less powerful when it comes to asking for help. God stands ready and waiting for us to call upon His strength to get us through the trial, and we would be surprised at the number of friends and family who are willing to be His instruments if we simply humble ourselves and admit our need.

2. Get proper treatment and medication - Proverbs 17:22 "A cheerful heart is good medicine, but a crushed spirit dries up the bones."

Much of depression is a result of chemical imbalance in our system. Consequently, it is very difficult to have a cheerful heart even in the midst of what would appear to others as a reason to be joyous and celebratory. When our spirits, bodies, and minds are in despair, we shrivel up like dry bones, and if we do not get proper diagnosis, treatment, and medication, we will destroy ourselves and possibly all with whom we come in contact.

It is imperative that people with bipolar disorder seek out a doctor who is qualified to diagnose and treat the illness and that the patient understand the need to administer the correct dosage at the appropriate time.

3. Understand your disorder - Psalm 139:13-14 "For you created my inmost being; you knit me together in my mother's womb. I praise You because I am fearfully and wonderfully made; your works are wonderful, I know that full well."

The Psalmist tells us that God knows everything about us even before we were conceived in our mother's womb. We can't possibly know ourselves the way that God know us, but through our trials He reveals Himself to us and us to ourselves and provides us with ways of understanding our hidden nature. With His strength and power and with the help of your doctor, you begin to know the triggers that set off your bouts of depression and your manic highs and can learn to control your reaction to them.

I came to learn that I was wildly excited as basketball season approached and entered each one with high hopes and sometimes grandiose expectations. At the end of the season, regardless of the success we had attained, I was often thrown into the depths of depression and often would stay there until the next season began. I always looked forward to the fall and dreaded the spring. Once my "beast" had a name and I came to recognize the cyclic pattern of my disorder, I was prepared for the emotions that came with it and was better able to control my reaction. Understanding bipolar disease took away the confusion about my behavior in certain situations and was a key turning point in my recovery.

4. Find an accountability partner - James 5:16 – "Therefore confess your sins to each other and pray for each other so that you may be healed. The prayer of a righteous man is powerful and effective."

Even though one has admitted the need for help, has received the proper diagnosis and treatment, and has begun to understand the disease, the bipolar disorder is still in existence. Each time it makes itself apparent, it would be very easy to let old emotions, actions, and insecurities rise to the surface, and start blaming others, once again, for everything that is going wrong in our lives. That is the reason it is so important to find someone you can trust to hold you accountable and at the same time not judge you for your problems.

You should choose someone who is not too close to the situation so that the accountability partner can be objective in listening and advising. The person you choose should be strong in character, wise in judgment, and someone who will tell you the truth even if it is hard to hear. And it probably goes without saying that the person you choose should be of the same gender so that you have the same perspective on certain issues and so that your relationship doesn't lead to other problems.

5. Discipline yourself - I Peter 5:8 "Be self-controlled and alert. Your enemy the devil prowls around like a roaring lion looking for someone to devour."

Until I knew what had been causing me to feel and act the way I did, I always thought that I was being attacked by some sort of beast and that I was powerless against it. Once I knew its name, had learned more about it, had received medication to fight against it, and had found someone to talk to about it, I knew that it was my responsibility to finally take control.

I had always been very disciplined when it came to training for basketball and to practicing my piano and violin, but never very disciplined in guarding my tongue or stopping my gambling, smoking, or drinking addictions. I came to learn that certain situations triggered these reactions, and

I had to discipline myself to avoid those situations even though they were harmless for the people with whom I liked to spend my time. Not being able to take part in activities that others enjoy without any harmful side effects is probably the hardest part of my bipolar disorder. It's fairly easy to remember to take my medication, to meet with my accountability partner and therapist, and talk about some of my issues with the people who love and support me, but it's very hard to discipline myself when it comes to doing some of the things I really love doing but things I know will trigger negative reactions.

Sometimes you will find that all it takes is a deep breath to gain control, other times you need to remove yourself from the situation, and all the time you rely on Christ to provide an escape from the temptation. Whatever the means, a person with bipolar disorder must take some responsibility for his reactions and stop blaming everyone else.

6. Accentuate the positive - Philippians 4:8 "Finally, brothers, whatever is true, whatever is noble, whatever is right, whatever is pure, whatever is lovely, whatever is admirable - if anything is excellent or praiseworthy- think about such things."

It is as important to control your thoughts in the same way that you control your actions. You have heard of the phrase, "garbage in, garbage out." The phrase reminds us that whatever we put into our minds and bodies is eventually what comes out of them. If we constantly eat unhealthy food, we will become unhealthy, and if we constantly think negative thoughts we will only think in negative terms. We all have things in our lives that we are ashamed of, been in situations where we were embarrassed, done things that seem unforgivable. If we meditate on these negatives, we will never move forward. Rather we should focus on the times when we did that which was right or successful, look at the good within ourselves, learn to love and respect the person whom God created us to be.

When people with bipolar disorder are in a depressed state, the negative is all that they can see. When I find myself thinking that nothing I do is right or good, I write post-it notes to myself and put them in prominent places, like a mirror or the dashboard of my car, maybe on the refrigerator. These notes remind me of who I am in God's eyes: I am fearfully and wonderfully made; I can do all things through Christ who strengthens me; in Christ, I am a new creation. When I recall what God sees in me, I gain a peace about my situation, and I begin to see the present and future in a new light. When we cast all of our negative thoughts on God, we can count on Him to turn them into positives.

7. Seek counsel - Isaiah 28:29 "All this also comes from the Lord Almighty, wonderful in counsel and magnificent in wisdom."

When I first learned that I had bipolar disorder, I needed help in understanding the disease and help in treating it. With my parents' help I found a counselor in the doctor who also treated me. I continue to counsel with him from time to time. He was vital in saving my marriage: he helped Alicia and me to share our concerns with each other; he taught us how to talk to each other and how to accept each other's negative and positive traits.

I also found it important to talk to others who were struggling with some of the same issues I was dealing with. These people became my support group. They help me to see that I am not the only one with problems. They remind me of where I have been and how much better I am doing. They keep me on track with my medications and behaviors.

I am thankful for these people in my life, but I know that the only counselor I can always count on is God. He is the One who gives me comfort in my trials and wisdom in my need. I can always find whatever advice I need in His word. I discipline myself to read and study His word daily, and from that I derive the strength I need to face my disorder and to overcome its control of my life.

8.   Release the guilt and forgive yourself – I John 1:9 "If we confess our sins, He is faithful and just and will forgive us our sins and purify us from all unrighteousness."

Forgiveness is a difficult concept for sinful human beings to grasp. As humans we believe in justice and punishment for wrongdoing. We can't conceive that anyone would be willing to erase the wrongdoing and let the punishment slide. When we don't receive the punishment we think we deserve, we feel guilty, and that feeling hounds us each moment of the day.

The bipolar person lives in a world of guilt, for his sins, his failures, his lack of self-esteem, his inability to accept responsibility, the pain he has caused others, and the list continues. The guilt wreaks havoc in his life and only leads to more wrongs and more guilt. The only way to get rid of the guilt is to confess it, and the hardest person to confess it to, and consequently to receive forgiveness from, is the person himself.

Forgiveness is best demonstrated at the cross where God's justice and mercy meet. Because God is Holy He must punish sin, but because He is also Love, He is merciful and forgives the sin through Christ's substitutionary work on the Cross. We don't deserve God's forgiveness. It is His love gift to us. All we need to do is accept it, and we are free from all guilt and shame.

Because we have been forgiven, we are commanded to forgive. Nothing that we have done or left undone is too big for God to forgive and, if that is true, then nothing is too big for us to forgive and that includes ourselves. God commands us to forgive ourselves. When we can do that, the guilt vanishes and we move on.

9. Memorize Scripture - II Timothy 3:16 "All Scripture is God-breathed and is useful for teaching, rebuking, correcting and training in righteousness."

The Bible is the Spirit-led Word of God. In it He tells us everything we need to know to live a holy and righteous life. It doesn't matter whether we are bipolar or emotionally stable, whether we come from functional or dysfunctional families, whether we are rich or poor, intellectual wizards or dunces, God loves us and wants us to know Him and to sanctify us in His image. The Bible is His instruction manual, and if we know it inside and out, forward and backward, it equips us to handle whatever Satan, "the beast," throws in our path. It derails all the emotions and behaviors of any mental illness. The Word of God alone is truth; it alone is where we find our salvation from all earthly trials.

10. Pray continuously - I Thessalonians 5:16-18 "Be joyful always; pray continually; give thanks in all circumstances, for this is God's will for you in Christ Jesus."

God loves us and wants to be in fellowship with us always. He knows our every need and He stands ready to fulfill it. He wants us to lay all our cares on Him. He answers every prayer; it may not be the answer we thought we wanted, but it is the answer that is always best.

There are many times when I pray that it seems that things get worse instead of better, and I question what God is doing or if He is even listening to me. I have come to know, however, that what He has planned for me is so much better than what I was asking for, that my prayer was almost placing God in a box. My prayer was so limited that I wasn't even tapping in to God's power or the riches that He had in store for me. I have come to know that His plans for me are for my good and that the trials that He allows me to go through are to make me dependent upon Him and no one else, especially myself.

Prayer needs to be a constant in the life of all of God's children no matter where they find themselves in life's circumstances. Prayer keeps us in communion with the One who loves us beyond anything we can imagine. We are the apple of His eye. He is focused on us and if we are focused on Him, we will never be disappointed. If we are focused on Him, our dreams will change, they will be according to His will, and He will give us the desires of our heart. He will cure all of our diseases. And He will be glorified.